9. 95

Home Port VICTORIA

Home Port

*A collection of true stories of
men and ships that sailed from this port,
told by old seamen at meetings of
the Thermopylae Club, Victoria, B.C.,
including short sketches of their
narrators, articles on relevant history
of the Port of Victoria, and two maps.*

VICTORIA

*Editing and
background writing*

by

URSULA JUPP

Dust jacket painting of ship Thermopylae
by J. W. Hardcastle
photographed by Ann Wilson

DESIGNED AND PRINTED BY THE MORRISS PRINTING COMPANY LTD., VICTORIA, B.C.

Dedication

This book is dedicated to all the brave men who have sailed out of the Port of Victoria, and particularly to those who related their adventures and life at the Thermopylae Club and so laid the foundation for its publication.

Acknowledgements

BEHIND THE PUBLICATION of this book lies the co-operation of many. To them I would express my gratitude.

... to the Thermopylae Club for permission to use its records and to the many Shipmates therein who have helped in ways too numerous to mention;

... to the staffs of the Provincial Archives and of the Reference Room at the Greater Victoria Public Library who have unfailingly and cheerfully responded to my appeals for help;

... and, last but not least, to those several seamen, not at present Thermopylae shipmates, who have so patiently searched their memories for some link missing in the story of one or another of the tellers of the yarns in this book;

... to all my most grateful thanks, and a hope that they will at least find some recompense in the reading of these old tales of the Port of Victoria.

The poems, "Say That He Loved Old Ships," page 57, written by Daniel Whitehead Hickey, "The Ocean," by John Augustus Shea, page 72, and "Ocean," by Robert Pollock, page 109, are reprinted by permission of Coward-McCann from *The Eternal Sea* by William M. Williamson; Copyright 1946 by Coward-McCann, Inc.

Foreword

THE LOVELY CITY OF Victoria was founded by those men and women who travelled around Cape Horn in the tall ships of the last century. They brought with them their culture, their skills, and their tools. Many of the men were sailors bent on following the sea from a new port on what was, in those days, almost a new sea.

Like London, Copenhagen, Amsterdam, and Bristol, Victoria brings her ships into the city, and before the days of steam, the lower yards of the ships would overhang the streets. So Victoria is a sailor's town, and its citizens are seldom out of sight of the sea.

The sailing traditions of the city have been preserved by the Thermopylae Club, which once numbered many Cape Horn sailors among its members. Alas their ranks are getting thin, and the art of story-telling is almost lost.

Ursula Jupp is a member of the Thermopylae Club, and its historian. She has worked hard and long in this, Canada's Centennial Year, to record for the generation which flies now and pays later, the endurance, skill, and humour, of the old Victoria sailors.

May this book enjoy fair weather and a soldier's wind.

ATHOLE GRAHAM CONING, *Master*,
The Thermopylae Club, Victoria, B.C.

Contents

HOME PORT: VICTORIA, B.C.

*From here many men have sailed out
into the implacable Pacific. Two craft hold a
unique place in her registry of shipping.*

SINCE THE ESTABLISHMENT in Victoria of a Registry of Shipping hundreds, perhaps thousands, of vessels have headed out Juan de Fuca Strait bearing below their stern-name the words VICTORIA, B.C.

Today over 1,150 so identified carry the name of Victoria up and down the Pacific coast, and beyond. Most are classified under such types as ferries, coastal freighters, commercial fish-boats or, possibly, private yachts.

Sixty to eighty years ago the greatest number of registered vessels would have been sealing schooners, those dauntless little boats that, each Spring, left Victoria's snug Inner Harbour to spend months in the waters of the Bering Sea or around Japan. Of these there were well over a hundred.

But there have also been on the register of the Port of Victoria two mavericks, craft which in each case has been "only one of its kind."

Today it is the great water-borne oil drilling rig, SEDCO135 F, that has this honour. In the early 1890's it was the ship *Thermopylae* whose bulk towered (though less spectacularly!) at Ogden Point and was the only "full-rigged sailing ship" ever to call Victoria "Home port."

Victoria today is home port to thousands of seamen, both active and retired. In the latter category are not only those who have served along this coast, but also many others for whom, in their sea-going days, home port was London, Liverpool or some other far-away seaport.

It is hard now to say how long ago it was that the first of these retiring master mariners came to take up his residence in the city

15

that was his choice out of the wide range that a long life at sea had laid before him, but over the years he has been followed by many others. All these immigrants soon found that they were not the only seamen in Victoria, that here before them were already settled men of the various maritime services that provided for the needs of the lengthy coast of British Columbia.

Together they formed a sizable group and from it came most of the thirteen men who on Trafalgar Day, 1932 met at the home of a man widely-known in Victoria for his interest in maritime and naval history — Major F. V. Longstaff.

The evening was spent in looking at a collection of slides of old warships provided by their host but, before they parted, the idea had come up (probably sparked by news reports of the founding of the Cutty Sark Club in Winnipeg) that it would be nice to meet like this more often — say once a month — and chin together over old times at sea.

Sure enough, the next month they did come together again, and at this first regular get-together chose for their group the name of the famous tea-clipper *Thermopylae*, a choice made not only in tribute to her proud record, but also because this vessel had, during the latter part of her career, been registered at the port of Victoria while she plied between this city and the Orient.

Of this original nucleus not one is now alive but Jack Kemp, a son of one of them, still recalls being taken as a small boy to one of those long-ago meetings at which old salts spun yarns of their years at sea.

"They sat around a long table. It all looked so dim; I think they just used candles to light them," is how the son of Fred Kemp (one of whose yarns appear in this book) remembers it.

The details may not be accurate but the atmosphere is there — the friendly casualness, the attempt to recreate the remembered companionship of meetings in dim cabins in far ports of the world in years long past. This was the heart of the meetings when, in the 1930's, men with memories of decades on the deep gathered in their retirement to yarn together.

Today the big table is gone, the seats are arranged in rows and bright lights burn overhead, yet still that comfortable amiability and informality permeates the club.

Yet there are some forms and traditions. Today, even as in 1932, the monthly Dog-watch starts at the striking of Eight bells. Behind the head table sits the worthy "afterguard" — skipper, purser, first and second mates and supercargo. Members of the "crew" are addressed as Shipmate and among them are to be found Bosun, Ship's Writer, Carpenter and Cook, and even, since a weak moment in 1954, Stewardesses.

Today the ship's complement comes from a widely-varied background, ranging from the man or woman who, though never having been to sea dreams often of it, through commercial fishermen, ex-naval officers, ship chandlers and builders, up to those honoured doyens of the club, the men who in their time have clawed their way under sail round the obdurate Horn itself.

Thirty years ago the gatherings were composed almost entirely of true deep-sea sailors. Many had fifty or more sea-years behind them, and when in those days the call was made, "Anybody with a yarn?" who knew what tale might not come from memories that totalled well over five hundred years, perhaps even a thousand?

It is decades now since the first shipmate rose to his feet to share with fellow seamen memories of his days at sea, days when oceans were wide, communications few and sail still the major source of power.

After him came many others.

Though many of the yarns they told were just that, unpremediated musings told and forgotten, others with tales to tell, dubious perhaps of their ability as extempore speakers, or anxious to have the details all correct, brought their stories in manuscript form and, at the end of the meeting, deposited them in care of the club.

In doing this they, all unconsciously, became tools of the history of a crucial period in the sea's story for these "ancient mariners" made up a unique group. These were the men who had been at sea in a time of great change; men who had served when the natural power of sail had almost ruled the sea; who had lived through the years of experiment when they saw beautiful ships sullied by the insertion of those "hideous contraptions," steam engines (though still at first the masts that flanked the belching funnel carried some sail to soothe minds not yet ready to put full trust in the fiery boilers). At the last they had seen sail almost driven from the sea by the new invention.

The formation of the club through which, as it happened, their stories of these changing times were saved, came none too soon for only too often and sadly, during its first ten years, the veterans stood in silent tribute to yet another octogenarian who would come no more to share his yarns with them.

But still the manuscripts accumulated in the old cardboard box. As the Thermopylae Club had no settled berth of its own, care of these archives passed unrecorded from hand to hand . . . until came the discomfitting time a few years ago when it was found that no one knew where they were!

Somehow, somewhere, sometime, someone had taken the box for safekeeping, ill-health perhaps intervened, and now the irreplaceable records were missing.

Their recovery came about in a way typical of this city where retirement turns all trades into gardeners.

Walking one day along a suburban street, one of the more recent members paused to compliment a man on the garden in which he was working. Garden talk led to ship talk . . . and on to the discovery that the gardener was a lapsed member of the Thermopylae Club (perhaps one of those unfortunates precluded by his "ticker" from climbing the stairs to a second-storey meeting-place) and to his recollection that in the dim recess of some cupboard in his house lay the long-lost box of yarns!

Following this recovery a committee was set up to check the stories for authenticity, and to prepare them for publication. They endeavoured, as far as possible, to leave the tales as they were written, any additions only those demanded for clarity. However, the reader is asked to keep in mind that in most cases these men not only had no aspiration to be writers but also, and more important, speaking as they were to fellow-seamen, the tendency was more to play down the danger of their experiences than to dramatize them.

The "pace" too of the tales may seem over-leisurely to inhabitants of today's jet age, yet this gait was only what appeared natural and seemly to men who had lived most of their lives in a world when, to get from London to Victoria in 109 days was a *swift* journey!

Nevertheless one matchless virtue they do possess — Truth. The unvarnished, unadorned but unmistakeable flavour of first-hand experience.

In order, in this Centennial year, to make this book a truly Canadian one, it has been decided to publish only those stories (with one amusing exception!) that deal with ships of this coast. It is planned to publish the remaining stories next year.

18

LOSS OF THE OSCAR

by CAPTAIN A. MCDONALD

To gain some idea of the extreme danger of the disaster described so calmly below and the courage displayed by McDonald when he "crawled back to the wheel-house," an account of the explosion abstracted from the following day's Nanaimo Free Press *follows McDonald's story.*

IN JANUARY 1913 I was on the small freighter *Oscar* carrying a full load of dynamite and ordinary gun-powder from the powder works at Telegraph Bay, near Ten-Mile Point, to the Britannia Mines when the vessel caught fire in the engine-room. We were then off Protection Island, near the small town of Nanaimo, Vancouver Island.

The fireman instead of getting help at once tried to extinguish the fire first himself and it was only when too late that I, master and part owner of the vessel, knew of the trouble.

I at once altered course for Protection Island in order to give all hands a chance to get away before the ship blew up. (And to soften the damage to Nanaimo).

Soon the whole ship was on fire and the wheel-house had to be left, the wheel first steadied so the *Oscar* would go on to the beach.

All hands gathered right forward so as to jump as soon as possible. But then I noticed that the ship was not keeping her course so I had to crawl back to the wheel-house to steady the ship again! By this time the cases containing the dynamite were on fire. . . . The course was steadied and soon the vessel struck a rocky part of the shore and all got safely off the deck, the chief engineer and myself being the last to go.

(At this point McDonald omits telling a part of the story that admirers remember. On the shore was a woman stunned by this sudden and terrifying intrusion on a quiet beach. McDonald paused to pick her up, threw her over his shoulder and carried her away from the danger of explosion.)

On shore, the engineer and I got down in a small hollow where we threw ourselves on the snow-covered ground.

Suddenly there was a terrific explosion!

When I recovered my senses and cleared my face from snow and moss I stood up and looked around. Seeing the chief on the ground, I called out to him and wanted to go to him but found I had lost the use of my legs. I could stand but I could not walk. After a few minutes control of my legs returned.

I then went over to the chief engineer, shook him up, and found he had had the same experience — he could stand but could not walk.

Later in the day we were picked up by a fisherman who had been eight miles away when the explosion took place and the concussion had splintered the glass in his wheel-house and done other minor damage.

McDonald's crew on this trip consisted of: Albert Edge, 1st mate; George Donaldson, chief engineer; Thos. Rankin, fireman; Geo. Layton, deckhand and Charlie Wung, cook.

*   *   *

While McDonald and his crew lay in the snow, what was happening in Nanaimo?

According to the next day's paper the startling flash of blinding white light and the succeeding blast roused in thudding hearts fear of an explosion in the mines or at the powder works. Then as glass began to crash from almost every window in downtown stores and horses to bolt in panic, streets were filled with pedestrians striving to avoid one danger or the other. Mercifully although there were many cuts only one was serious. A few hours had to pass before the cause of all the damage and confusion was discovered.

At the scene of the explosion the *Oscar* herself, recently the kindly home of six seamen, was reduced to debris so fragmented that the sea looked like soup, and even her boiler was never found. So monstrous was the force of the blast that a launch nine miles away had its bow blown off!

CAPTAIN ALEXANDER McDONALD,
FIRST SKIPPER OF
THE THERMOPYLAE CLUB

WHEN, AFTER THE EXPLOSION on the *Oscar*, Alexander McDonald surveyed the debris-strewn waters around Protection Island it is not likely he then recalled another time when he had also seen the sea abob with flotsam, nor paused to consider that great as had been the explosion on the *Oscar* it could have been but as a pin dropping compared with the montrous blast behind that earlier flotsam.

That sight had been in 1883, the year of the eruption on the Indonesian island of Krakatoa when waves 50 feet high took the lives of 35,000 and did not completely lose their force until they reached Cape Horn, over seven thousand miles away!

This was the year when seven and a half year old Alec took with his father, master of the *City of Corinth*, a sixteen-month voyage to Australia and the Orient.

It was, of course, some weeks after this disaster that the *Corinth* sailed into its area and young McDonald, awakened by a strange whispering sound outside the hull against which his bunk was built, went on deck to find the ship surrounded by acres of bobbing lava. This, in the days before wireless, was the first hint they had of some great unknown cataclysm.

Had he been on deck an hour earlier the boy too would have heard the cry that caused the masthead lookout to be accused of drunkenness. "Ice ahead!"

Sea ice within five miles of the Equator! . . . but what sailor, young or old, had ever before seen, or even heard of, floating lava in the quantities they encountered then?

Fifty years after this Alexander McDonald was to meet, at the

Thermopylae Club, Captain Frank Wilson and hear that he had been in that area then too, his first awareness that anything was wrong his inability to find the lighthouse at the entry to the Straits of Sunda.

At times McDonald would relate other recollections of this youthful voyage at club meetings. Most poignant of these, and one whose details he clearly remembered half a century later, was the loss by drowning of one of the *Corinth*'s young apprentices . . . the lengthy attempt at rescue, and finally the accompanying of his solemn-faced father to his cabin where the record of the tragedy was entered in the log-book, which the mate was then sombrely requested to sign.

In 1890 McDonald himself became an apprentice. By 1900 he had earned his foreign-going master's ticket, then shipped for two years as mate on the *Ardencraig*.

Then marriage and six years on the London-New Zealand run before they moved to Victoria. Here he served first with the British Columbia Coast Steamship Service, later on small coastal freighters.

Finally came the position that, while it gave him the opportunity to be for lengthy periods near his wife and the family that now numbered four daughters, also allowed him to spend weeks, sometimes months, on the deep ocean he loved so much. This was as navigating officer on the cable-ship *Restorer*, the vessel that kept in repair the cable from Bamfield, on the west coast of Vancouver Island, to Guam.

Shortly after his retirement from this came the formation of the Thermopylae Club, and his election as first skipper.

Alexander McDonald was a gifted and spell-binding speaker. Penetrating eyes burned beneath striking black brows and from a mouth full and sensitive as a poet's poured stories that brought to the meetings a sense of romance never since equalled. And herein lies the rub, for Alexander McDonald had no need to write out his stories and sadly few of his reminiscences are to be found in the club's Archives.

MY EARLY DAYS

by CAPTAIN A. MCDONALD

I WAS BORN and brought up in the village of Kincardine, situated on the north bank of the river Forth, Scotland. As a child I put most of my spare time in sailing around the reaches of the Forth.

Needless to say I had no boat of my own at that age, but I was not backward in asking for the loan of one which I knew I could handle. These local boats were all fitted with a standing lugsail and made a good weatherly course. As I grew older they got tame and I wanted something more interesting and exciting. I was now between seven and eight years old.

Well, my father's ship would be arriving in London shortly from Calcutta (or maybe Bombay) and I would get my mother to ask him if he would take me on a voyage.

When it got near time for him to arrive my mother and I went up to London (we had heard when the ship had been reported passing St. Catherine's on the Start) and we met her just as she was entering London Dock.

I can hardly express my feelings when, that fine morning, I boarded my father's ship, the full-rigged *City of Corinth*. Sailors were at this time busy unbending the sails and stowing them away in the sail locker. How busy I was taking stock of everything; so busy that although I heard my mother ask my father if I could go on the next voyage I don't remember what he said at the time.

The able seamen looked like pirates; they all had beards and carried a big knife in a leather sheath attached to a belt around their middle. It was summer time and they were mostly bare-footed.

I also got down in the half deck among the apprentices. They had no beards but they carried the same kind of knife in their middles. I did not know then how essential an open knife was when aloft.

Next day I was again on board. What a change had taken place! No bearded sailors about, but a rough lot of stevedores had taken their place and were busy hoisting bags of rice and bales of jute on to the wharf.

After quite a long while (so it seemed to me) the ship was ready to sail again. Evidently my mother had been promised that I would be taken along for my people took me up to Gardiners, a big out-fitters store in Aldgate where I was given a miniature outfit just like a sailor's; heavy clothes for cold weather, white for the tropics.

Eventually sailing day came. I said good-bye to my mother. Poor soul, she was crying when I stepped aboard with my father. The gangway was pulled on board and the last lines cast off. With a towboat ahead we passed out of London Dock when crowds of people saw us off for we had passengers aboard, bound for Sydney, Australia.

Imagine, if you can reader, what an exciting time a boy of seven and a half years was having. Well I remember the tug that let us go off Beachy Head lighthouse, the wind strong on our port side, sail after sail being set and sometimes two sails at once.

At last the good ship *City of Corinth* was on her way.

ONE CHANCE IN A THOUSAND

by CAPTAIN A. MCDONALD

THE NARRATIVE which follows is one told me by a well-known deep-sea fisherman, resident of Victoria, B.C., and, as will appear later, it goes to show how the deep water men had reason to dread Vancouver Island's rugged west coast.

It should be recorded that this fisherman had been engaged by the well-known firm Findlay, Durham and Brodie, canners of salmon in earlier days, date of our story being 1900. He was to explore the coast of the vicinity mentioned in this article with a view to finding out and recommending a site that might be suitable for a canning factory or purse seine fishing ground.

On accepting the firm's offer, he took passage in one of the steamers of the old C.P. Navigation Company, disembarking at Alberni. There he procured an Indian canoe and the necessary provisions for an extended survey of all the bays, islands and inlets adjacent to Barkley Sound.

Following an examination of the most likely prospects of the Alberni Canal and Effingham Inlet they were held up for more than a week in Toquart Harbour by a sequence of violent S.E. gales. Now in the Sound proper, they had reached the northwest corner.

When the weather had moderated they proceeded with the work in hand, and early one morning while paddling past Hand Island they sighted a barque, apparently at anchor. Nearing her, they made out her name to be the *Highland Light*. By this time they judged that the ship was unmanageable, as all her sails were hanging in rags along every yard. They also noted that the crew was working at the pumps.

On coming alongside they hailed two rough unshaven men who

were leaning over the taffrail. What, they asked, was the barque doing in such a place, and how had she got into the Sound without striking something?

On such points the sailors were ignorant, though they knew they were driven in by gale after gale since they had cast off the tugboat at Tatoosh Light. Their sails had been blown away, and they had not the slightest idea of their true position.

They said the captain with five of his men had left the ship early that morning with one of the boats, to look for assistance. Also to find out, if they could, where they had brought up. The only chart they had on board was one on a small scale, extending from Lower California to Alaska, utterly useless in their present plight.

After some time the captain returned with the men in the boat after a fruitless search for either human or habitation. He had landed probably just about the spot where the Sechart Whaling Station now stands. On seeing the canoe with strangers alongside his vessel and noting that one of them was a white man, he was overjoyed. His imperfect knowledge of the coast, apart from ports of call, had left him with visions of Indians with murderous intent, also piracy and pillage. Now he found they were true friends when the need came.

When apprised that his barque was about as far up Barkley Sound as it would be possible to get, even under the most favourable conditions, he was astounded, realizing that she had drifted and been blown into her present position on a long dark winter's night, in a southeast gale coupled with driving rain. Unknowingly he had passed the Starlight and Black Rock Reefs, and the Great Bank extending three and a half miles, each a mass of roaring waters breaking to tremendous heights. He had also threaded through and between all the islands, and yet it seemed that not a man of her crew had ever known of the imminent dangers they and their ship had escaped.

The skipper lost no time in asking the fisherman to make all haste and despatch a telegram and, as acknowledgement of the service so rendered, to accept the sum of twenty-five dollars.

The offer was appreciated. The canoe reached Alberni in good time and carried out its mission so promptly that the next day the tug *Lorne* was on her way down to the barque.

The *Highland Light* was taken in tow, and without mishap on the trip, arrived at Esquimalt. Here leaking badly from her unpiloted journey from Tatoosh to the high reaches of Barkley Sound, she was put into dry dock.

Her voyage, as originally arranged, was from Puget Sound to San Francisco. Knowing, as we do, how many good ships have been lost off the west coast of Vancouver Island, in spite of the most seamanlike efforts to keep them offshore and avoid disaster, this story is only the more remarkable. Of it one may truly say, "Just another instance of the strange things that happen at sea."

(In the following year — 1901 — the *Highland Light* foundered off Estevan Point about seventy miles northwest of the scene of her earlier escape. No lives were lost.)

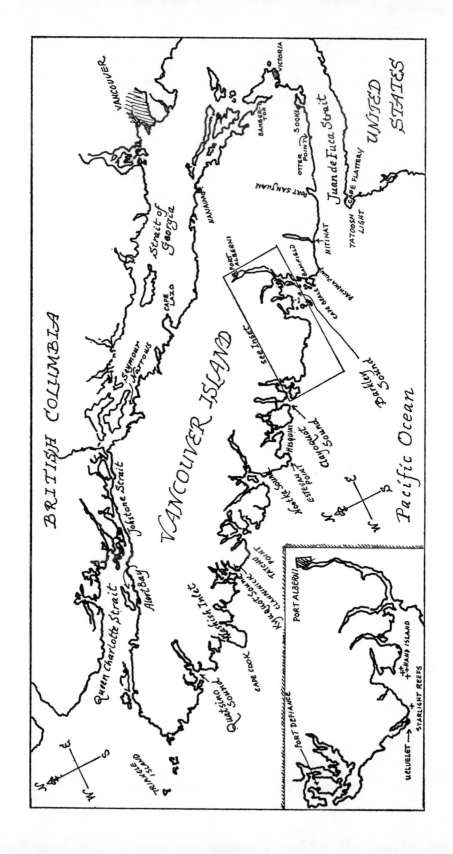

CAPTAIN J. J. MOORE

Look at the picture of J. J. Moore at the age of around 27 or visit today* (1966) the 98-year-old Captain Moore who sits gleefully, and without glasses, watching a wrestling match on T.V., and the same phrase springs to mind, "A broth of a boy!"

And sure enough he had to be!

Though bearing an Irish name and heart, he was born on the Isle of Man. Afloat and off on the trawlers to the fishing grounds of Iceland and Greenland by the time he was thirteen, he early knew that life was a harsh business.

Till he was thirty-five he remained in these rough seas, but a man in whose veins ran the blood from the line that produced Fletcher Christian (leader of the mutiny on the *Bounty*), could not forever remain deaf to the call of far seas — especially if he has a wife also ambitious — and in the early 1900's the couple took the then big step of moving to the Pacific coast.

One of Joseph Moore's earliest positions here was on the tug *William Joliffe*, a very powerful vessel, built originally for Liverpool owners to compete in the race for tows in the days when large numbers of sailing ships were still docking there. But, in operation, the hoped-for champion proved too costly and when a visiting Victoria ship-owner cast envious eyes on a vessel he thought capable of coping with the storms of Vancouver Island's west coast a deal was soon made.

In 1907 she arrived here and began to drive her twelve-foot propellors through Pacific waters. When Moore first served on her she was still privately-owned. Later he was also an officer on her

*Captain J. J. Moore died in late 1966 at the age of 99.

when she was employed by the Federal government as a Fisheries Protection boat.

From the *Joliffe* he moved to another Federal service, the Hydrographic Survey, a nice tidy scientific term that cloaks a life that, especially in pre-radar days, could be decidedly uncomfortable and dangerous — and still has its perils. On the British Columbia coast especially, the vessels that have to chart waters of rapidly alternating depths, and near-the-surface pinnacles, lead a life of perpetual anxiety.

For his first ten years at this work J. J. Moore was mate, then master, of the *Lilloet*. From her he moved to the new *William J. Stewart*, remaining with her as master till he was over seventy-five.

Well can the nonagenarian boast with an Irish twinkle in his eye, "I know every nook and cranny on this coast." After forty years among them, he should.

ROUGH WEATHER ON A
WEST COAST PATROL

by CAPTAIN J. J. MOORE

DURING THE YEAR 1912 towards the end of October, the *William Joliffe*, Captain Tommy Thomson, was commissioned as a Fishery Protection Cruiser and patrol ship on the British Columbia coast. About this time Commander C. P. Edwards of the Radio-Telegraph Branch was making one of his periodical inspection trips to the coast wireless stations, and the *William Joliffe* was detailed to carry him.

At the time the *William Joliffe* was not equipped with wireless, and as Mr. Edwards was a strong advocate of wireless communication, he issued instructions for the installation of an emergency transmitter and receiver on the ship.

We left Victoria at midnight in dirty weather and succeeded in making a landing at Pachena Point the next day. The following day a landing was made at Estevan Point and then the ship was headed for Triangle Island. The weather had been getting steadily worse and Triangle Island reported no possibility of landing there. We went into Quatsino Sound for shelter and Triangle Island was asked to furnish a weather report in the morning.

During the night the weather got worse and by morning a howling S.E. gale was blowing. All hands aboard started cleaning up guns and counting shotgun shells for here we were, near Winter Harbour, a hunters' paradise for duck and geese, with a howling southeaster and no possibility of landing on Triangle Island. All preparations were made for a good day's hunting under ideal conditions, boats were made ready and everybody got into hunting togs.

We were going to hunt later, but not, as it turned out, the kind of hunting we were figuring on.

Just about the time we were all ready to start, Mr. Edwards

31

decided to give Triangle Island a call and advise them that we were remaining in shelter till the weather moderated. Then the bomb exploded!

Triangle Island advised us that they had been trying to get in touch with us as the C.P.R. West Coast steamer *Tees* had sent out an S.O.S. call for assistance, but no further particulars could be obtained before the wireless set on the *Tees* had apparently failed.

The *Tees* was known to be somewhere near Kyoquot Sound, and it was feared the ship had struck one of the bad reefs near the entrance.

Skipper Tommy Thomson consulted with the late Captain Holmes Newcombe, who was then the Fishery Officer of the ship, and it was decided that the hunt must start immediately, not for ducks but for the *Tees*.

When the *William Joliffe* headed out from the snug harbour into the full force of the southeaster we knew we were in for a bad time. The weather was so thick and dirty, it resembled a thick fog and was what is known on the coast as a "full black southeaster." A heavy sea was running at the time, and as the *William Joliffe* headed into it she was doing everything but turn over for we were driving full speed. Green seas were coming over the bows, but after one sea carried away a deck ventilator and another one bent part of the bridge rail, the ship was run at reduced speed.

We made 26 miles in six hours and at dusk we were about three miles east of Solander Island, Cape Cook. There was nothing for it but to heave to for the night.

And what a night! No fires in the galley, pots and pans rolling on the galley floor, broken crockery strewn everywhere. The Chinese cook and the white mess boy were locked in each others' arms on the mess-room floor, one praying in Chinese, the other in English. In normal times these were deadly enemies and always fighting! When asked how he felt the cook replied, "Oh, I think I die."

Next morning we looked into Mr. Edwards' cabin where the wireless set was located, and what a mess was there too!

A tool box had broken loose and the contents strewn all over the cabin floor, together with a miscellaneous collection of books, papers and other articles. A bookshelf had emptied its contents into Mr. Edwards' bunk and he was surrounded by books and papers. An Army revolver had come to rest near his head, with several boxes of cartridges. His first words were, "Oh, good Lord, what a night!"

The weather had not improved and it was still very thick but an attempt was made to locate our position by running close in shore. The first sight of land was a glimpse of Solander Island through the thick haze. We passed Solander no less than six times during our trip and Captain Thomson was heard to remark, "Well, I think I will know that pile of rock next time I catch sight of it."

We again lost sight of land and the next indication we had when we headed in was the lookout shouting, "Breakers ahead!" We pulled out again and sighted the S.S. *Salvor* also out looking for the *Tees*. We both anchored in Klashish Inlet for the night.

The following day the weather had cleared and we made Kyuquot Buoy where we sighted the life-boat from the *Tees* in which were First Officer Thompson and four men. When we picked them up we were told that they had been trying to get around Tatchu Point to try and deliver a message to advertise their position, as the wireless set on the *Tees* was not in good order. They stated that the *Tees* had broken her propellor and damaged her rudder, and was tied up about fifteen miles up the Inlet.

When we reached the *Tees* we found her tied up to the trees in a sheltered spot and everyone well and happy.

The position of the *Tees* was not a good one for the sending and receiving of wireless signals. She was close under the shadow of high hills and the signals from the reduced power of her transmitter were only partly picked up on the first night of her mishap. Although coast stations were in constant touch with the *William Joliffe*, no word could be received from the *Tees* due to the screening of the hills.

Owing to the uncertainty of her condition, the outside world was getting anxious and many urgent messages were sent asking us to make further efforts to find her.

Under present day conditions, with the improved transmitters and receivers now in use, these anxious conditions would not exist and there would be a number of ships and coast stations able to get in touch with her even behind the hills.

HARD WORK — AND ALL LOST!

by CAPTAIN J. J. MOORE

In 1912 I had the following experience on the *William Joliffe*.

We left Esquimalt about the twentieth of November and proceeded to the west coast, weather not very good, wind blowing a succession of gales from the S.E. to S.W. Towards dark on the first day we anchored in a little bay called Clanninick. Next morning about 7 a.m. weighed and proceeded towards Cape Cook, when about 8 a.m. we sighted a vessel about 8 or 10 miles away, and, changing our course stood over to her and found her to be the sailing vessel *E. K. Wood* of San Francisco loaded with lumber.

She was in a bad plight, sails all blown away, mast carried away, and apparently water-logged. The crew were leaving her. We took them on board, twelve of them, and they were glad to get on board our ship as the coast around there is a very wild one, and it is doubtful if they could have effected a landing. Tried to get their boat on board our ship, but owing to the heavy seas it was smashed to pieces and we had to let it go.

Next question, what to do with the ship? Our skipper, Captain Thomson and the fishery officer, Captain Newcombe, reckoned nothing could be done now that their tender had been smashed and only a small flat-bottomed boat belonging to us was left.

I thought I could make it if I could get anyone to help me but they were at first not inclined to let me try. But as one of the crew volunteered, it was decided at last that I should have a try, along with the second mate of the *E. K. Wood*.

Everything was got ready and, getting the tug as close as possible, we launched our little boat. The wreck at this time was very low in the water, the poop and forecastle head being the only two places dry. We managed to scramble on board and, making our little boat fast astern, a line was got on board the tug and away we started. But after towing about a quarter of an hour the line broke. Another was got on board. This was very hard work for two men. It was then about ten o'clock in the morning and blowing hard.

The ship was badly wrecked, two of her masts being gone and her mizzen-mast loose, swinging about twenty feet each time she would roll. Her deck cargo had been washed overboard and her main deck was almost awash. My volunteer and I were taking turns steering, and while he was steering I went below for a look around.

What a sad dreary sight it was! The water had been right up in the cabin before she had lost her deck cargo overboard and socks and shirts and other articles of clothing were floating around or stuck in all kinds of places.

The day gradually wore on. We did not make much headway, the weather being bad, and about 3 p.m. Captain Thomson signalled that we were long enough on board for that day and to try to get back to the tug. The *Joliffe* then stopped and our little duck-boat, by now capsized, had to be got ready. We got the boat turned around, but there were no oars or a bailer, so my volunteer went down into the cabin and got two bunkboards from which he shaped two oars, and I found a small saucepan to use as a bailer.

We managed to empty the boat, got into it, and I taking the oars, and my partner bailing for dear life, we started for the *Joliffe*. Sometimes we could see the ships, but when in the trough of the sea they were lost to sight. Halfway towards our goal along came a huge breaker curling up ready to break over and swallow us up. I kept the boat head on to it and managed to keep in front of it till it broke.

We got back to the *Joliffe* again and began towing, but after about half an hour the towrope parted again and we had to leave the ship to her fate, and run back to Clanninick to anchor.

Next morning when we went out to take her in tow again we could see no signs of her, and although we cruised around looking everywhere we never saw her again nor was she ever heard of. None of her cargo was ever found. We had the crew with us and that was, after all, the main thing.

We took them to Alert Bay. They were later sent back home and Captain Thomson and Captain Newcombe each got a pair of binoculars from the American government for services rendered.

35

BEN AXHORN

THE EXISTENCE OF CLUBS such as the Thermopylae sometimes leads to surprising meetings. As when new shipmate Ben Axhorn found that the club's skipper, Captain Alexander McDonald was the son of the Captain McDonald under whom he had signed his first ship's articles in Sydney, Australia in 1886. And more, that the *City of Corinth* which he then joined was the same vessel on which three years earlier young Alec had taken his first youthful journey.

Axhorn's first voyage on the *Corinth* was but the first of the many and varied that lay behind him when he settled in Victoria. And even after retirement he was not finished with the water, going then to spend two years on yet another type of craft — the dredge *Mudlark*, then engaged in deepening Victoria's Inner Harbour.

Asked why he had joined this outfit, Axhorn had a neat reply. "Well," he said, "you know how the sea grows on you. When it calls you have to answer!"

In the old box of yarns were several from his nimble pen.

His story of the *Tythonus*, and White's of the *Hutton Hall* that follows illustrate two different aspects of that temptation so often encountered on lengthy voyages of the days of sail — the broaching of cargo.

BROACH — BUT DO NOT SELL

Perhaps, if the Captain had not wanted a feather-bed, all would have been well!

by BEN AXHORN

IN AUGUST 1889, I arrived in Victoria on the Liverpool barque *Tythonus*. We were very short-handed when we arrived at this Canadian port so were towed around by the tug *Sea Lion* and moored stern on by the Custom House.

By the latter part of October we had taken on our cargo, 52,000 case of salmon, and then went to anchor in Royal Roads, while we looked for men to complete our crew.

We wanted two — a cook and a mate. As there were no mates in Victoria our skipper had, after a lot of negotiating, got one in San Francisco to come later on. A cook was asking $50 a month, which was just the salary the captain was getting, while the second mate's pay was $25. To give a cook $50 was unthinkable so the steward proposed to put me in the galley. This solved the cook problem.

At last our skipper got a wire — the mate had left for Victoria.

On November 8th the Frisco boat arrived and our skipper was on hand with a buggy (there were no autos or street-cars in those days) to bring the new man to Esquimalt. By the time they came aboard the tug *Pilot* had come around, so all was ready to sail. Soon it was, "Man the windlass!" the skipper taking charge on the forecastle head.

We got the anchor up, the hawser aboard, and the next morning were being let go off Flattery. The *Pilot* came under our quarter, took the last papers for shore and left us. A light northerly wind was blowing which gave us a good run offshore and a chance to get everything stowed away and lashed down.

After the day's work, the steward came along to the galley and told me to see everything secure before turning in as the glass was going down.

It was breezing up now, so we had to shorten her down until we had her in lower topsails, main and foresails. Later we took in the main and foresails and lay to under the two lower topsails. We were just wallowing in it helpless.

No one turned in that night. Eight bells struck, lookout and wheel relieved, so I went to the galley to get coffee ready by two bells. The weather being too bad for the lookout on the foc'sle head, he had got on the galley, holding on to the mainstay just above the galley door which was half open on the lee side. I was stoking up the fire when the lookout yelled out, "Doc, come up." I jumped up and saw a vessel heading straight for us, leaping over the combers like a greyhound.

I thought, "This is the end."

On she came, running light under main topgallant sails, her side lights showing up fine. Nearer and nearer she came. She was going to run right over us when a miracle of seamanship happened. They had seen us and as she rounded up and cleared our quarter we could have got on board her. Had we been ship-rigged our yards on the mizzen would have locked together. She just missed us. You could not have put a cork fender between us.

After a while, with a good fair wind we got down to warmer weather. Now the two watches seemed to vie with each other in keeping their respective rigging in good shape; the mate's watch the foremast and head gear, the second mate's the main and mizzen. I know of no better situation than a good ship in fair weather with a good fair wind. Everyone seemed to be happy and content.

Most sailors have some kind of hobby. Some make models, others mats, and in various other ways amuse themselves.

The steward one day said to me, "What do you think — the old man has a hobby? Bet you can't guess what it is.

"He is getting Sails to make a canvas bed-tick and is going to fill it with feathers. You will soon see."

I saw. A baited hook was thrown over the stern, a gunny-bird grabbed it, was hauled aboard, killed, plucked and thrown overboard. This was kept up till the mattress was complete. Dire consequences were prophecied on account of what to the seamen seemed an act of sacrilege, and though still the fair wind held, the men's spirits seemed to have been dampened by the killing of the birds.

We made Cape Horn 67 days out.

It was the custom to make the skysail fast every night (we carried a main skysail) and set at daybreak — of course weather permitting. One morning the boy sent up to loose it counted twelve sails on the horizon, all homeward bound. We made the thirteenth. In the latitude of the River Plate we met our nemesis.

It was early morning, clear as a bell; no indications of a blow. We were going along with royals set, when, like a shot from a gun, down came the pampero.

"Call all hands. Clew up the fore and main royals, t'gallant sails, everything."

We might just as well have done nothing. In as short a time as it takes to record it we were running before it stripped of everything but the skysail and fore and aft sails.

It was then one heard, "Yes, I knew it would come sooner or later," but what a mess with all our heavy weather sails gone.

That night the breeze went down with the sun. We got no other blow that passage.

Next morning all hands began clearing up, beginning at the fore. There was not much left to send down, just cut away the rovings on the jack-stay, pull it clear of the fore and aft stays, stand from under, let go!

That day finished the fore; the following day the main underwent the same process. Our sail locker was empty with the exception of two old spare topsails. All hands were glad when the job was finished.

From then on we got three kinds of wind. Light winds, head winds and no wind.

Leaving Esquimalt we had stores calculated for 140 days, and it did not look as if we would make it in 150 unless some great change for the better took place. We were now out 120 days, position about Lat. 5°N., Long. 28°W.

Where were the North East trades? We needed them badly. There was quite a lot of whistling for the breeze, but none came. Even the skysail was not taken in at nights; no afternoon watch below.

Now too the stores were going down; everything was pretty well gone; even the hardtack was getting low, so a can of salmon from the cargo was served out each day per man. For some this was to lead to trouble.

Yet still we were making slow progress and all hands were getting weary and discontented, when the old man decided to run for Fayal in the Azores if we got the right wind. This we did, about 150 days out. It was a good breeze and under all sail we ran into a bay, our signals flying.

A boat came out and took an order for stores to come off next morning. As night was coming on we stood offshore, intending to run in at daybreak, but while we were dodging around a ten-knot S.W. breeze sprang up with every indication of staying with us.

"Call all hands aft. Men, we have a good breeze which, if it holds, will take us in in five or six days. Let us carry on and get it over. I will give each man two cans of salmon a day."

All agreed. "Let her go while she feels like it. Square the main yard. N.N.E." Everyone was jubilant.

It lasted just two days.

Fourteen days later we made the Channel with a good breeze but foggy. We picked up our pilot. Surely we shall make it this time.

Getting up towards our goal the usual bum-boats came along for whatever there was to dispose of but we had nothing — till a bright idea struck someone! There was quite an accumulation of salmon in the foc'sle.

"It's ours. Let us sell it to the boatman."

They did but as the boat dropped astern the old man from the poop saw the cans in the boat. He began to walk up and down very fast, doing some tall thinking — but he never said a word.

Next morning the tug came alongside and we were soon in the dock, 168 days out. Even as the mate said, "Belay all, that will do, men," two policemen came aboard, and read out the names of those wanted, the charge being mutiny.

Then the Board of Trade runner stepped in and went security for them. In the end they were fined £5 each. To give the old man his just dues, if they had not sold the salmon he would have let it pass.

*　　*　　*

Just before leaving Esquimalt the barque *George*, Captain W. Grant, came down from Moodyville with lumber laden for London. We half expected to hear that she had arrived ahead of us. Mr. Duncan, our old mate, was mate of her. Three weeks later I got a letter from the steward: "Barque *George* towing up, 180 days out."

They too had missed the trades.

 J. B. WHITE

SENIOR MEMBER of the Thermopylae Club and one of the few remaining who have rounded the Horn under sail is J. B. White who
joined the crew in November 1933. Thirty-five years earlier he had
signed on with his first ship. Not all these years had been in the
merchant service, or even at sea, for in 1911 Jack White had settled
ashore in Victoria, the port that had been his destination on that
first-ever voyage on the *Hutton Hall.*

Then came 1914 and on August 5th the ex-sailor reported to
Esquimalt for service with the Navy. He did not leave this service
until well into 1919, behind him then the experience of being on
the *Thunderer* at the Battle of Jutland, beside the *Vanguard* when
she blew up at Scapa Flow.

BROACHING THE BRANDY

In the end they were 8532 bottles short!

by J. B. WHITE

ON MY FIRST VOYAGE, January 1898, on the ship *Hutton Hall* we loaded general cargo in Salt House Dock, Liverpool. There was a large consignment of Hennessy 3 Star Cognac, also beer and wines. As it came about, by the time we reached our destination, Esquimalt, B.C., this part of the cargo was considerably smaller! Even during the loading stevedores broke open some of the cases.

We were towed out by the *William Joliffe* at four o'clock on the afternoon of Saturday, November the 5th.

There was a strong nor'wester blowing and we had a length of towing cable on the bight for towing. Most of the crew had been celebrating before leaving with the result that when, at six bells in the first watch, the mate gave orders to cast off the tug both ends were cast off. That finished the towing cable as far as we were concerned.

We soon ran out of the dirty weather, and the first Saturday the old man opened the slop chest. Some of the hands went in a little too deep to suit the skipper. He told them they wanted to get all they could and then desert the ship when we got to Esquimalt and go to the Klondyke — or "Klony" for short.

Included in the cargo were two cases of clay pipes and two of wax candles. Four weeks out most of the crew were smoking new clays, which need not signify anything, but I remember noticing it.

The mate was a nervous man and was suspicious with the result that he spoke to the old man about the crew being able to broach cargo, as the hatches were only battened down, but the old man assured him that it was all right.

Six weeks out we expected to pick up Staten Island, near Cape

Horn, but the wind, which was on our starboard quarter, fell to a light breeze, about three or four knots.

The mate had the first watch and he had a big Dutchman in it called Neuman. He had the first trick at the wheel. While the mate was pacing the poop he twice noticed Neuman take his hand away from his mouth and put it in his overcoat pocket.

He made a couple of turns, when he noticed the same thing again. When he got aft he looked in Neuman's face but after a few moments decided there was nothing wrong. He was on the point of moving away again when Neuman put his hand in his pocket and pulled out a quart bottle of "Henney" and invited the mate to have a drink!

In the morning watch strong bars were put on the hatches and locked with the handcuffs. Then the old man and the mate searched the fo'castle, finding eight and a half bottles of Hennessy's. The rest of the day the mates tried to find out who had been down and, naturally, nobody knew.

The wind during this time had fallen to almost a dead calm and we did not pick up the Staten Island light until six bells in the first watch. The old man having left orders to be called, the second mate did so but the old man had been having a quiet evening with the Hennessy. He just grunted on seeing the light and went below again.

Next morning we were abeam of Staten Island with no wind. In the afternoon watch we were in the same position but closer inshore so it was decided to take some soundings. They showed 16 fathoms. When we were hauling in the line, a seaman in the mate's watch named Wysmore or "Santos," came on deck full of Hennessy and insisted on helping to heave the lead.

This incident proved that the crew did still have access to the cargo, which worried the afterguard as they knew the weather conditions would not last.

A few days later when we came on deck one afternoon an Irishman named Doherty showed signs of having had some Hennessy. A little while after the second mate wanted to go aft to see how things were and he gave orders for nobody to go into the fo'castle, especially Doherty.

Soon after he left, Doherty did go to the fo'castle. The second mate returned before he did and, of course, missed him so the second mate went to the fo'castle too. As he entered it, so Doherty came up the port side. He was asked if he had seen the second mate.

He said, "No," but that he had run into trouble. When asked what, this is what he told us.

"When I got in the fo'castle I thought I saw Santos looking under the bottom bunk, so I gave him a hard crack on the stern sheets and asked him where he got 'Klony's' slippers from.

"He backed out and it was the old man himself!" Santos had a pair of pants the same as the old man's.

He got out quick.

Soon the second mate came for'ard and saw Doherty.

"Where were you just now?"

"I've been here all the time, Sir."

"Like hell you were. Did you see the old man?"

Doherty gave a sheepish grin and told the second mate what had happened, who had to smile, serious as it was.

About the tenth day we got a fair slant and headed north. A raid was made on the fo'castle nearly every day. Sometimes Hennesssy was found, sometimes not.

We had a fore and aft bridge and one Sunday during the morning watch the second mate took a walk for'ard on the bridge. As he reached the break of the fo'castle he noticed the coal locker hatch was off and the head and shoulders of a man sticking out from under the combings.

The mystery was solved. It was Neuman, his face covered with blood and coal dust. The hatch was put under lock as the others and from then on there was no more Hennessy.

Eventually we dropped anchor in Esquimalt 137 days out. The *Leavenbank* and *Foyledale* were also there. After discharging government stores, we towed around to the Outer Wharf where trouble again showed up.

One night the mate took a walk for'ard about 10 o'clock and surprised Santos at the fore hatch with a line down and another man below. Santos disappeared quick. The mate looked down below and saw Neuman with a case of Hennessy bent on the line. He put the hatch on and said he would get the police and went aft. He returned about twenty minutes later but Neuman was gone. When the hands turned to in the morning, the two of them had disappeared.

Altogether, in the end, we were short 237 cases (three dozen bottles to the case)!

From Victoria we went to Vancouver, then to Seattle to load flour for Hong Kong. The mill supplied the ship with several hundred new sacks to re-bag any broken ones. Some of the flour was taken for ship's stores.

We arrived in Hong Kong 72 days out. The *Simla* was there, having been dismasted in a typhoon.

While discharging all hands were down below re-bagging broken and damaged sacks. We made an extra one out of about ten to make up for the shortage.

A month later we left in ballast for the Columbia River but got caught in a typhoon the night we left, and it was three weeks before we sighted Formosa. From then on we had good weather until we crossed the Meridian. Then we got it for six weeks. One month under a goose-wing mizzen lower topsail, the rest blown away.

Eventually we reached the river, took on a pilot, but he would not take us over the bar so we stood out again. The night was foggy and about eight bells in the last dog a ship's mast headlights loomed up on our starboard bow. We backed the main yard and the ships passed close enough to read the names.

It was the *Scottish Isles*, 175 days from Panama!

Next day we crossed the bar, towed to Portland and loaded wheat for the U.K. Left Astoria New Year's Day and arrived off Queenstown where we got orders for Antwerp.

The sailmaker, who joined us in Portland, was happy at this as his mother lived there and he had not seen her for thirty years.

During the afternoon the old man shortened her down to tops'ls. The sailmaker, being happy, went aloft to help. He went on the lower yard to pass the gasket round the clue; somehow he slipped and fell off the yard, striking a backstay which turned him inboard, so that he fell in front of the galley door.

He was dead when we picked him up. We buried him at sea the next day.

We sailed up the Channel as far as Dungeness where the *Titan*, a Dutch tug, took us and towed us to Antwerp, 157 days from Portland.

So ended my first voyage.

ONE GROUP OF SEAMEN who warmly welcomed the start of the Thermopylae Club in 1932 was made up of men, some active, others retired, from the British Columbia Coast Steamship Service, a service now very reduced but at that time employing a sizable fleet of a score or more vessels on the British Columbia coast.

Most of the skippers in this company in those days had served in sail, and they rejoiced in the opportunity the monthly meetings gave them to travel once more in memory with men who had shared long ago the life of the open ocean.

Of the B.C.C.S.S. men even the youngest, Captain George A. Thomson, still in 1967 an active member of the Thermopylae Club, served his apprenticeship in sail — four years on the barque *Gulf Stream* taking him many times around dangerous Cape Horn.

After this came some years on "tramp" steamers but with the First War he was back at the Cape again, this time on H.M.S. *Orbita* as she patrolled in search of Count von Luckner's deadly *Seeadler*.

In 1927 he came to this coast to join the B.C.C.S.S. and spent thirty years with it, during these bringing out six of the company's new ships from British shipyards.

Considerably older than Thomson were Captain C. P. Kinney and Captain C. Sainty. Sainty left no story of these waters, but of unique interest to Victorians and all who value the canoe *Tilikum* is the story of his meeting in mid-ocean with the canoe and its famous captain near the end of their historic voyage.

Sainty was master of the ship *Port Sonachan* at the time, one of the mere handful of vessels met by Voss during his 40,000-mile journey.

46

To quote Captain Sainty: "While commanding the *Port Sonachan* I saw what I thought was a ship's boat in the North Atlantic. We squared away to see what it was. It was *Tilikum* looking very trim with topsides painted white enamel and gold leaf cut with blue." (This would be from the work done in Pernambuco.) "Voss and his mate, a fine young man, came aboard. He was ninety miles out in his longitude, his chronometer being a nickel railroad watch. They had dinner, a drink, and presently Voss asked for a bath.

"Voss and his mate stayed on board and were towed to the latitude off St. Michael's when he went off, but returned at once with a broken lower rudder pintle which we repaired. Then he made off."

Captain C. P. Kinney's story of his command of the *Senator* covers more than three years and takes him as many times out of, and back to Juan de Fuca Strait.

This other veteran began a life at sea possibly even earlier than Captain Sainty for it was in 1868, the year the *Thermopylae* herself was launched, that twelve-year-old Kinney was first afloat. Such a youthful initiation into sea-life was not unusual in his Nova Scotian birthplace for the rocky Maritimes set their children early on the stern path that was to make them the men of courage and integrity for whom this land is noted. Charles Kinney, throughout his long life, never let this image down.

From 1868 until 1910 most of his time was spent in sailing ships. Sometimes he was accompanied by his wife and with them their gradually growing family. Sometimes the only companionship they could have was through letters. Letters in which news of the voyage was lightened by anecdotes of the pets he carried — two dogs, parrots and, incredible as it may sound but vouched for by his daughter, rats! Ordinary rats . . . though Captain Kinney's rodent friends had had their teeth filed down before being allowed the freedom of his cabin . . . and his shoulder, where, as he wrote, they often perched.

Sometimes reports of his doings appeared in the papers, such as when in 1889 as master of the ship *Mary Burrill* he took out the first load of grain to leave Seattle.

Years later public acclaim and the press once more met this captain when he arrived in Victoria with the powerful tug *Salvage King*, fresh from the builders in Britain.

At the Thermopylae Club there were many to appreciate the stories of these B.C.C.S.S. men.

LUCK...OR NOT?

*Three times he took the ship Senator
out of Puget Sound on world voyages*

by CAPTAIN C. P. KINNEY

I WONDER IF ANY OF YOU believe in luck? ... that is, a lucky or unlucky ship, a lucky or unlucky day, or lucky or unlucky anything? Possibly what I have to say may set some of you thinking.

In March 1904, I received a cable from C. E. DeWolf and Co. of Liverpool, G.B., asking me if I would go to Port Townsend, on Puget Sound, and take charge of their ship *Senator.* I replied in the affirmative, and on March 9th I left my home in Yarmouth, Nova Scotia for Port Townsend, Washington, by the Canadian Pacific Railway.

All went well till in the vicinity of Lake Superior when a broken rail caused four cars to go off the tracks and turn over on their sides. They were dragged some distance in the deep snow. I escaped injury by inches only because I was going through the train when it happened and had just stepped off the car when the first went off the track.

I arrived in Port Townsend on the morning of the 17th and found the ship ready for sea. On going on board I found that on the previous voyage four persons had died on the ship. The first officer had died in Port Elizabeth, South Africa, and on the passage from there to Sydney the captain's wife had died. The ship loaded coal for Cebu, Philippine Islands and after discharging there sailed for Puget Sound. On this passage the new first officer had died. The ship was ordered to Bellingham to load and before being ready for sea the captain died. I think he must have died of a broken heart.

The ship being ready for sea, crew and everything on board, we proceeded down Juan de Fuca Strait in tow of the tug *Pioneer* at 6:30 p.m. on the same day I arrived in Port Townsend.

The next day, the weather being bad, the tug took us into Clallam Bay where we anchored. On the twenty-first we were still lying in Clallam Bay when one of the sailors developed smallpox.

We took the usual precautions, put the man in a room by himself and burnt some of his things and thoroughly fumigated the seamen's quarters.

On the 23rd, the weather being favourable, we proceeded to sea in tow of another tug, the *Wanderer*. I did not report the illness. You can imagine the anxious hours waiting and watching but fortunately no more cases developed. Nursing the patient myself, cream of tartar was the only remedy I gave him. Some years before, my wife was with me on another ship and she saw the remedy in a paper and cut it out and gave it to me, and I believed it to be a cure for the malady.

From Cape Flattery to the Equator we had the usual weather and crossed the Line in 125°W., 27 days out. On May 4th we sighted Pitcairn Island. On nearing it, we hove to and two boats' crews came on board bringing fruit and vegetables to exchange for sundry articles. Clothes were what they wanted most. They reported the number of people on the island to be 150 and in good health. A president is elected every New Year and everyone, male and female, 17 years old or over, is entitled to a vote.

From there we had the usual weather until reaching Lat. 56°S., Long. 72°W. when we took a hard westerly gale. I will quote one entry in my log: "June 9th comes in with a heavy westerly gale with thick snow. Midnight, hard squalls with snow. Have been obliged to run with wind on starboard quarter in order to safely clear Diego Ramirez. Have had no observations for several days and our position uncertain." "June 10th: Strong gale but weather clearing. 10 a.m. sighted Diego Ramirez, bearing N by E, about 12 miles."

After passing Cape Horn we had a lot of easterly wind, nothing of note happening. Arrived at Port Natal after a passage of 127 days. Rather a long passage but after arriving found that other ships had been longer, which was some consolation.

The next jinx happened in Port Natal. The ship was moored to dolphins with bow to the pier, and discharged lumber over the bow. Just after the last piece had been discharged a heavy squall struck us bringing a heavy strain on the stern moorings which carried away the dolphin to which the stern lines led, allowing the ship's stern to swing around and collide with a steamer, doing slight damage to her and badly twisting our own rudder stock.

As there was nothing to get a line to, I was obliged to engage a tug boat to hold us against the wind all night.

The ship was judged liable for £400, payable for damage done to the harbour works. After going to the dock and making repairs and cleaning and painting, I gave the bonds and sailed for Newcastle, N.S.W. I will just mention here that I did not pay the £400, as I put the case in the lawyer's hands and won it. I intended going into dock to clean and paint but as I was obliged to go for rudder repairs I made an insurance job of it all.

Nothing of note happened on the passage of 35 days to Newcastle. We loaded there with coal for Honolulu and sailed on December 18th.

The first officer, though a capable man, acted queerly at times — he had been wounded in the head in the Boer War. During the passage on one occasion while the ship was hove to in a hard gale he kept the ship away before it, with the yards braced up and was loosing the upper main topsail when I came on deck. The men were called down from aloft and the yards squared in. In the meantime the ship was shipping heavy water. The mate on being questioned could give no explanation for doing this and I do not think he knew what he was doing.

After a boisterous passage of 75 days we arrived at Honolulu. After discharging we were delayed three days on account of two deserting seamen.

Got orders to proceed to Royal Roads for orders and sailed March 19th. Arrived in Royal Roads after a passage of 25 days where we discharged ballast and trimmed what remained on board. On the 25th of April took tug *Lorne* and proceeded to Vancouver. Moored at Hastings Mill wharf; began loading on May 1st and finished on the 31st.

From June 1st to 13th waiting for a crew. Succeeded in getting all but one man and decided to go one short. On the 13th, which was Friday, got tug and pilot and went to the ship and found that the second officer had deserted and all the crew but one man had refused duty (jinx).

The Boatswain was promoted to second officer and with the two officers, three apprentices and one man, assisted by longshoremen, got the anchor up and towline aboard and sailed.

50

On the 14th the seamen decided they would go to work even on an empty stomach and make sail. Then we fed them.

Passed out from Cape Flattery late this day and crossed the Equator in 125°W. 27 days out. All went well till reaching 34°S. when the main topsail tie carried away, letting the yard come down by the run, and it, carrying away the lifts, came down on the lower topsail yard, carrying away the supports on that yard, then both yards came down across the mainstay and held there by the sails (jinx).

Got the yards up and secured to the mast and sent down the broken ironwork. For four days the swell was too bad to do anything. Then got rolling chocks made and secured, and the next day all repairs made and set sail. From then on had usual hard gales but nothing more of note happened until September 4th in Lat. 57°S., Long. 72°W. when we got a hard gale from the northwest, hauling westerly and southwest with high sea. Put ship on port tack. At 11 p.m. the gale had increased to hurricane force, the ship labouring heavily and shipping much water as she took heavy lee rolls. Oil was distributed from oil bags.

As I had had but little rest for several days, I lay down on a settee without removing my oilskins and at about 11:30 p.m. something awoke me with a start. I rushed on deck and inquired of the first officer who was on watch if he had heard anything or anyone calling and he replied that he had not.

At that time it was lightning very sharp and not being satisfied, and guided by the lightning, I felt my way forward over the deck-load to where the lookout was on the forward house and asked him if he had reported anything and he said the starboard light was out.

I started to go aft again when in an unusually bright flash of lightning I saw something was wrong with the lee side of the deck-load. On investigating, I found that it was washing away and that the lee bulwarks had carried away from the fore-rigging to the after part of the main rigging, apparently some of the wreckage was hanging to the lee fore braces. After securing the yards with heavy lines, the braces were cut with much difficulty. A large chisel was lashed to a long pole and when the ship rolled to windward, the braces would be slashed, until finally we got them clear.

Also we had to cut away a spare spar which was hanging by one lashing, the other end being overboard, and the main rigging being in danger of being carried away by it. At daybreak the gale had moderated somewhat. Then we got clear of the wreckage and got the braces rove off.

In the meantime a large portion of the lee side of the deckload had gone overboard and since it was impossible to secure it, I deemed it prudent to jettison what was left, which was done and finished at 7 p.m.

The officers then suggested we put back to Valparaiso but I told them that we could get to Falkland Islands sooner, but instead of making for there I kept south till, far east of them, I informed them we were bound for East London, South Africa, our destination.

Nothing else of note occurred till September 30th when the second mate fell overboard. At the time we were running with square yards and making about five knots. The ship was immediately brought to wind and the starboard lifeboat in charge of the first officer was put out. They picked up the second officer and were back on board again in 35 minutes.

That was the last jinx for this passage and we arrived at East London on November 6th after a passage of 146 days.

I asked to be relieved, and received a reply at the next port which said that I was doing fine, that the ship had always gone sideways and I was not to expect anything else.

After discharging cargo and making repairs, we sailed on December 6th for Semaphore, South Australia and arrived there after an uneventful passage of 33 days. Got orders to proceed to Smokey Bay in the Great Australian Bight to load wheat. I was obliged to get extra water tanks as no water was to be had at Smokey Bay. On being ready to sail, the crew refused to go to sea and demanded a survey of the ship. This was instigated by parties interested in the Charter Party, I found out afterwards. In consequence I had to take the ship to Port Adelaide. This took time as there was no drydock there and was obliged to tip the ship by shifting the ballast. Consequently I lost the charter, which was a very good one and as grain freights had gone down, I was ordered to Newcastle, N.S.W. to load coal for Acapulco, Mexico.

Arrived at Newcastle, April 20th, after a passage of 20 days.

After some delay in getting clear of ballast as there was a large number of ships waiting for berths, we loaded coal and sailed for Acapulco on July 3rd and after an uneventful passage of 90 days arrived there.

Had quite a lot of trouble with the crew while there, caused by drunkenness and I was laid up with malarial fever twice, the last time when we expected to sail the next day, but did not do so till December 13th.

On passage nearly all the crew were down with malarial fever. Arrived off Cape Flattery 62 days out. Took tug *Dolphin*, but wind increasing, the tug could not handle us. Took us into Clallam Bay where we anchored till the fifteenth when the tug towed us to Royal Roads. While discharging ballast a man fell into the hold, but was not badly hurt.

After discharging and trimming ballast we towed to Quartermaster Harbour and went in dock to clean and paint and then proceeded to St. Paul Mill, Tacoma to load lumber for Valparaiso. Finished loading April 6th and after waiting a month for a crew, took tug *Lorne* and proceeded to sea. Arrived at Valparaiso after a passage of 92 days.

Anchored in outer Roads waiting for discharging berth, and while lying there one of the seamen shot another in a quarrel. More troubles!

After discharging part of the cargo we arranged to take the balance to Caleta Coloso, Chile for £250. We arrived there December 25th. Discharged the balance of the cargo and took in ballast after waiting two weeks for it.

Sailed for Royal Roads February 21st and arrived there after a passage of 77 days.

No freights offering, took the ship into Esquimalt Harbour when, after lying there for 14 months, I resigned command and as far as I am concerned, this ends the jinx.

But I would ask, "Is this luck or not?"

THE SHIP THERMOPYLAE, VICTORIA, B.C.

To HAVE BEEN the home port of one of those queens of the seas, the speedy tea clippers of the later half of the eighteenth century was an honour for any sea town. To have been able to claim, as Victoria could from 1891 to 1895, that on her port register was one of the two fastest ships afloat is an honour of which this city has perhaps never been sufficiently aware.

The question of whether it was *Thermopylae* or *Cutty Sark* that should have the pride of first place is one that even today is good for an argument in sailing circles but certainly at the time *Thermopylae* was berthed in Victoria there was one old veteran sailing ship captain who was not afraid to write in the local press of "the *Thermopylae* which, I believe, is still the fastest sailing ship afloat."

She was also beautiful . . . and she was glamorous, with an aura which rubbed off on to those who sailed on her so that they were said to be "not like other men."

Small wonder then that when a group of retired sailormen in Victoria looked for a name for their sea-lovers' club they decided to call it "The Thermopylae Club."

Many have written of this famous clipper, Basil Lubbock among them. "How sweetly she sailed!" he wrote, "able to fan along at seven knots in an air that would not extinguish a lighted candle," yet "she was both comfortable and easy to handle when running over 13 knots under all plain sail."

Even those she defeated applauded her. On her first passage, when she passed H.M.S. *Charybdis* off Port Phillips Heads, her captain hoisted the warm-hearted message, "Good-bye. You are too much for us. You are the finest model of a ship I ever saw. It does my heart good to look at you."

To use bald figures about such beauty seems sacrilegious, but then that is the practice of the day, so here in all their starkness they are: Length from stem to stern: 212 feet; Beam: 36 feet; Depth: 21 feet. Displacement when loaded: 970 tons. From keel to topside her hull was rock elm, above that India teak.

In rigging this vessel — planned to be a winner in the days when the earliest load of tea to reach London commanded the premium price — her builders made some changes from designs already in use. Mast height was lowered, sails widened, her mainyard a great 80-foot spar from which dropped a mainsail 40 feet deep at the bunt. Thirty-two hundred square feet of canvas in that sail alone!

The *Thermopylae* was built to make records — and she did, her speedy passages helped by her first captain, the daring, driving Kemball. It was under his command that, in the dim of early morning in November 1868, she left the London docks. By the time she returned to them she had broken many records, including making in one 24-hours 380 miles and cutting two days off the record for the Foo Chow, China to London run.

Thermopylae then was the talk of the docks.

It is rather sad to have to add that this record was not hers for long. Within two weeks the *Sir Lancelot* had shortened the passage by a further two days!

But the *Thermopylae* continued to pile up other records until rivals were driven to build the *Cutty Sark* to challenge her reign.

Finally it was steam that put an end to all sail in the tea trade and the ships moved to other uses. *Thermopylae* was sold to the Montreal firm of Reford who planned to use her on the Pacific to bring rice from the Orient to Puget Sound.

At midnight, on June 24, 1891, by the light of a moon just over full, she sailed for the first time up the Juan de Fuca Strait and anchored in Royal Roads.

Later, in Victoria, she was taken over by Nova Scotia-born Captain J. N. Winchester and had added to her crew a number of men from the sealing schooners, as well as three apprentices; Bob Spears, Harry Bilton and Frank Ferris, the last destined to become, during the First War, chief of the U.S. Maritime Commission. Among those in Victoria today who remember visiting the big ship in those days, and even climbing into her yards are today's centenarian Captain Charles Harris and the senior Mr. Wille at the bakery on Johnson Street.

On her runs to the Orient the *Thermopylae* had some rough times, the worst, that reported in the *Colonist* of March 24, 1892.

They arrived here 101 days after leaving Bangkok. Water spouts had menaced them and winds had been so destructive that Captain Winchester had felt he had to excuse his vessel's battered and untidy appearance when she reached Victoria with the words "though we left Bangkok with three suits of canvas, she now has not one presentable or serviceable sail!"

They had also run out of food and for the last ten days had been subsisting on rice, this while they were enduring two weeks of struggling to make the entrance into the Strait.

How different another voyage from China in a record 29 days!

In 1895 Victorians had their last sight of her cloud of white canvas coming up behind Race Rocks and she was once more off for Europe, this voyage being the only one, I believe, on which she rounded Cape Horn. In her holds then she had some of British Columbia's great forest harvest, including monstrous balks of Douglas fir, a hundred feet long and 24 inches square!

So ended Victoria's connection with a world-famous ship, a jewel in this city's history for long overlooked but now recalled by the plaque which the Thermopylae Club added to the Parade of Ships embedded on the Causeway wall in 1962.

"SAY THAT HE LOVED OLD SHIPS"

by DANIEL WHITEHEAD HICKEY

Say that he loved old ships; write nothing more
Upon the stone above his resting place;
And they who read will know he loved the roar
Of breakers white as starlight, shadow lace
Of purple twilights on a quiet sea,
First ridge of daybreak in a waiting sky,
The wings of gulls that beat eternally
And haunt old harbors with their silver cry.
Speak softly now, his heart has earned its rest,
This heart that knew each alien star by name,
Knew passion of the waves against his breast
When clouds swept down the sea and lightning's flame
Tore skies asunder with swift finger tips;
Write nothing more; say that "he loved old ships".

OF THE TWENTY-ODD MEN who "loved old ships" and formed in
Victoria in 1932 the Thermopylae Club to preserve their memory,
four deserve more than passing mention: Major F. V. Longstaff,
Captain George Kirkendale, Captain J. A. Philipsen and Captain
Alexander McDonald, the quartette who by their wisdom and
steadfastness helped to carry the club through its formative years;
years made difficult by the after-effects of the Depression and
further tried, during the Second World War, by the return to work
of a number of its scanty crew, elderly men who after a day's work
in the shipyards had little energy left to take them to a meeting in
the evening.

But somehow the meetings did carry on, the skipper during most of this time the dynamic Captain Alexander McDonald. This Scotsman, possessed of an almost mystical love of the sea and with a sense of drama that inspired others to see in their experiences unsuspected magic, gave the meetings life and meaning through years when the membership dwindled almost to the point of extinction.

In 1943 this quartette was joined by a fifth figure, a man who though resident in Winnipeg when the Thermopylae Club had its first meeting, must yet be counted among those influential in its start — Charles F. Gray.

II

That Major F. V. Longstaff, an officer retired from a British regiment and seldom seen on the streets of Victoria without the symbolic bowler hat, should have been prime mover in an organization devoted to the interests of the sea may seem at first surprising, but among the many interests of this vital man was a long-continuing research into naval and maritime history. But, originator though he was, the major held no master mariner's ticket and so was never able to fill the position of club Skipper. (Later this qualification had of necessity, to be abandoned.)

However this was not the case with the three who collaborated most closely with him as "founding fathers," Kirkendale and Philipsen particularly, who as Harbour Master and Assistant Harbour Master of the port of Victoria had a continuing and close connection with the maritime world. Of these two, more later.

And then there was Charles F. Gray. "Ah, yes, Charlie Gray!" they say, voices lifting even today in recollection of a man not easily forgotten.

To find where Charlie Gray fits into the list of those instrumental in the formation of the Thermopylae Club one has to turn to a day shortly before Christmas 1931, when the sight of a model of the *Cutty Sark*, displayed in a store window facing on Winnipeg's main street, brought this ex-mayor of the prairie city to an abrupt halt.

Suddenly he was once again that fourteen-year-old boy who had sailed as an apprentice on the old iron ship *Oronsay* in the 1890's. Spellbound he gazed at this reminder of a life far removed from the snowy prairies.

Then he thought, "Perhaps there are others too who remember the tall masts . . . ?"

A letter to the press from Charlie Gray, public figure and president of the association that encouraged the completion of the railroad to Hudson's Bay, drew wide attention and he received from within the city and other prairie points, sixty-five letters from longlonely shellbacks. In January 1931, seventeen of them sat down to dine together, and so was born the first of the Cutty Sark Clubs.

Later, other watches were formed in Calgary and Edmonton and and news of their founding inspired imitation as far away as Foo Chow. Articles on these clubs appeared in the press in various parts of Canada, including Victoria, where, in November 1932, the Thermopylae Club was formed. Hence Charlie Gray must be considered, if not a founding father, at least the club's godfather.

It was not until 1943 that Gray himself visited the club. He was then manager of Prince Robert House, a recreational centre for seamen during the war, and he became resident of Victoria and member of the Thermopylae Club for the rest of his life. In 1950 he became club skipper.

A vigorous, colourful, kindly man, Charlie Gray had behind him a varied career and one whose success he strongly and continuously attributed to his faith in a beneficient God. This was a faith that could well have had its birth on that dawn when, as a youth of seventeen, he sat in a lifeboat 500 miles from land and watched the *Oronsay* sink.

Even to the end that Higher Power was to be kind to Charlie Gray. Three weeks after he and his wife had had the pleasure and pride of travelling to Vancouver as guests of the Canadian Pacific Company and visiting the fine new P. & O. Orient liner *Oronsay* on her first visit to that port in 1954, he died quietly in his sleep.

These then were the men who gave leadership to the Thermopylae Club during the first half of its life. What of the rest of the crew of that era?

III

Of these some appear in this book along with the yarns they spun. Others told of voyages not properly to be included under "Home Port: Victoria" and slated to appear in another volume. But for the tellers themselves Victoria was indeed by now their home port and so they make a brief appearance here.

In honoured place among them stands Captain William Gregory, a member of the Honourable Company of Master Mariners and, as he wryly puts it, "eldest of the Younger Brethren of Trinity House, London."

Captain Gregory first went to sea in 1898 in the wool trade to Australia. Later he spent many years with the Royal Fleet Auxiliary Service. While in this he made several voyages to the Gulf of Mexico for the oil then just beginning to replace coal in the stokeholds. In connection with this Captain Gregory recalls the brightly-polished shovel, symbol of past toil, sometimes displayed on the quarterdeck of vessels that had "converted."

Captain Gregory is also one of the small handful of Cape Horners — men who have rounded that obstinate promotory under sail — in Victoria. Another is F. Walter Hearle, a Cornishman who, at the end of his years of apprenticeship, found plans for a career at sea totally frustrated by short sightedness. But the training of those early years later came in useful in the making of nets for the live-saving Carley floats in the Second World War.

Walter Hearle was also responsible for the rigging of a schooner once well-known around Victoria — Bill Tellier's *Black Dog.*

A very popular raconteur in the club was the late Lieut.-Cmdr. Nicholas Beketov, retired from the R.C.N. and also the Department of Transport, but once an officer in the Imperial Russian Navy. After the Russian Revolution he joined the White Russian forces and had many adventures in Asia and eastern Europe before coming to settle permanently in North America. In Victoria he was very devoted to the work of Gideon International.

One of the few Conway boys in the Thermopylae Club was Granville Cuppage, a man whose sea years, while short, added an intriguing, though macabre, tale to its Archives. But one voyage to Australia proved enough for Cuppage and the main part of his life was spent in British Columbia where he was associated with the Provincial Forestry Department in its earliest years.

That the sea, though abandoned as a career, still held an attraction is shown by his lengthy membership in Victoria's original Yacht Club. Now, as its sailing members fly the R.V.Y.C. pennant some may at times remember this man whose efforts obtained for that club its Royal Warrant.

Another amiable yarn spinner was H. W. Price, eight times around the Horn, but there were many others, equally long at sea, who left no written tale.

Prominent among the latter was Captain Harry Bilton, apprentice on the *Thermopylae* during the years she sailed out of Victoria. By the time Harry's apprenticeship was completed, opportunities of obtaining deck officers' positions on sailing ships were scarce and so most of his years at sea were spent in steam, on ships that served in the coastal waters of British Columbia. In 1944, after 22 years in command of the lighthouse tender *Estevan*, he retired ashore in Victoria.

Then in the Thermopylae Club Captain Harry Bilton found the congenial companionship of other ex-seamen, and at the monthly meetings his stalwart figure regularly filled one of the chairs in the front row, traditionally occupied by the seniors of the crew.

From those seats many have passed on . . . Captain A. Larsen, master of the *St. Roch* on her history-making voyage through the Northwest Passage . . . Captain A. M. Davies, that kindly old examiner for ticket . . . Captain Mathieson who used to take on his vessel soil in which to grow his own fresh vegetables . . . Fred Johnson . . . and many another whose names are not recorded in this book, but without whom the club could never have fulfilled its purpose as guardian of the memories of the sea and meeting place for old seamen.

ONLY NATIVE Victorian among early Thermopylae Club members was Oscar Scarf, who was born in Esquimalt in 1864 and spent all his life on this coast and the adjacent waters.

The first yarn he tells is of a maritime tragedy that once stunned Victoria.

It was on November 4th, 1875, that the steamship *Pacific*, loaded with nearly 300 passengers, set out from Victoria bound for San Francisco. A few hours later she was seen by a boy from the beach at Otter Point, and yet another few hours and she, and all but two aboard her, were lost, victims of a glancing blow from a sailing ship which after the collision, sped into the darkness unaware that the damage she had inflicted was of more than minor character. It was in fact to prove fatal.

For the sail-powered *Orpheus* indeed the main need seemed to be to attend to her own repairs, wasted effort as it turned out, for a few hours later she too became a total loss near Cape Beale on the west coast. However, fate was kinder to her for not a life was lost.

In Victoria the next day relatives and friends of the hundreds on the *Pacific* went peacefully about their business, unaware that those to whom they had yesterday waved good-bye were already corpses.

A storm on November 6th may have given them some concern, but by then surely the *Pacific* must be well off the coast.

To the boy at Otter Point the storm meant the chance of finding some flotsam on the beach, and so it was that the news of the wreck that was to shock Victoria was started on its way by a beachcombing ten-year-old boy — a boy who was later to become known as Captain Oscar Scarf, Sealer.

Probably no other member had memories that stretched so far back into the history of this coast as did those of Oscar Scarf. Even by the time the big square-riggers that brought White and McDonald to Victoria in the 1890's had sailed up the strait, Juan de Fuca had been for him familiar waters. Here from the decks of sealing schooners he had gazed up at many a ship, including probably even the *Thermopylae* herself.

But by 1905, after eleven harsh years in the North Pacific, he was ready for more amiable waters and moved to boats coasting around lower Vancouver Island and down to California. He was also, for a time, on the Dunsmuir yacht *Dolaura*.

Last of all "my boat" meant to Oscar Scarf the little launch in which he carried the mail across Brentwood Bay to Bamberton. By now it was the 1930's and he was also a member of the Thermopylae Club, and spinning yarns. The story of the *Pacific* follows immediately, another is in the section on sealing.

TRAGIC FIND OF BOY BEACHCOMBER

by CAPTAIN OSCAR SCARF

IN THE LATE SUMMER OF 1872 I left Esquimalt with two white men and some Indians in a large Indian canoe like the *Tilikum* and, after some delay on account of head winds, landed on the beach at Otter Point, 33 miles west of Victoria where the late Mr. Tugwell, with whom I lived, had a cabin and owned the land there.

I was just eight years old and did what little I could to help the men to build a new house one mile farther west. There I spent most of my time for the next ten years. It was while living there that with a friend, Indian Jonnie, we would look out to sea and wonder what could be at the other side of the great body of water, little dreaming of the strange things that were to happen to both of us on the other side and among the strange people we had never heard of at that time.

It was also while living there that I saw something that I shall never forget.

On November 4th, 1875, the steamer *Pacific*, outward bound with mail and nearly 300 passengers and crew, and the steamer *Salvador*, inward bound, passed, as many steamers did, about a mile off in front of our house. Each ship blew three whistles as they passed out of sight towards Cape Flattery, not thinking of course that of her passangers and crew few would see the light of another day.

That night the *Pacific* sank following a collision with a sailing ship off Cape Flattery. Only survivors were a Mr. Jelly who was found floating in a trunk and a Mr. Henly on a small raft some time later.

Though misty it was not bad weather but two nights later we

had a very heavy storm and, as usual, after a storm I went to the beach soon after daylight to pick up some pieces of timber that came up on the beach and might be useful on the farm. I was surprised to see a large ship's deck-house and part of a ship's deck breaking up in the heavy surf in front of our house.

I at once notified Mr. Tugwell who, after seeing the wreckage, sent a man on horseback with a letter to Mr. Michael Muir, the postmaster at Sooke, who in turn sent word of the wreck to Victoria.

The three mile beach from Otter Point to Muir Creek was covered with doors, buckets and life-belts plainly marked S.S. *Pacific*. We also found the golden eagle, a large gilded wooden eagle that the *Pacific* carried on her pilot-house. We sent it to Victoria and it was given to the owners of the *Pacific*.

On the beach at Otter Point, strange to say, no bodies from the *Pacific* were ever found though some were found near Victoria and San Juan Island.

ON THE TUG PILOT

by CAPTAIN OSCAR SCARF

ODDS AND ENDS OF MEMORY: Steam tug *Pilot* was built at Chemainus by Tom McDonald. I worked on the construction of the *Pilot* (which has split log facing to her deck buildings — see photograph) until she was ready for sea. Shipped as quartermaster with Captain John Butler (brother to Dan) and was soon mate. When Captain Butler left I was appointed master and served on her for thirteen years during which:

The *Pilot* picked up the *Ella Roleff* in distress in Blackfish Sound and towed her to Union Bay. Also picked up schooner *Eva* in distress in Milbank Sound and towed her into Seattle. Also picked up steamer *Cottage City* with broken shaft off Cape Lazo and towed her to Seattle.

Pilot pulled S.S. *Otter* off White Rocks; towed her to Ladysmith. Pulled big schooner yacht off beach at Oak Bay. Pulled S.S. *City of Seattle* off Trial Island.

Pilot also towed barge *Colorado* twice to San Francisco with coal and back to Victoria. Towed barge *Oregon* from San Francisco to Victoria. Towed three big scows from Victoria to St. Michael's at the mouth of the Yukon River.

In the two volumes that hold the records of Thermopylae Club "voyages" nearly four hundred pages are in the handwriting of but two men — the first 162 in the neat script of Captain J. A. Philipsen, Supercargo for the society's first six years, and later on, over 200 in the similarly uniform and legible hand of faithful long-time Purser Charles Tapping.

Both were men of office experience but otherwise their lives were profoundly dissimilar.

The first, Captain Philipsen, spent many years afloat. Born in the sea-girt country of Denmark he joined first the Danish Navy, but by the age of 16 had become an apprentice on the British-owned *Crown of Scotland* and, later, a naturalized Briton.

After obtaining his master's papers, voyages to the Orient showed opportunities ashore and he set up in Japan a stevedoring business with headquarters in Yokohama.

A few years after the great earthquake of 1924 he came to live in Victoria and, in retirement gave his time freely to the interests of the sea — coached young men for deck officers' certificates, worked with the Navy League and Sea Cadets — and helped found the Thermopylae Club.

With the outbreak of the Second World War he was back at sea again, delivering ships built on this coast to Britain and Australia. These missions completed and on shore again, he was soon engaged on work for the country of his adoption, giving lessons in navigation to young men training for the air at Patricia Bay.

But all these activities made a heavy demand on the heart of a man approaching seventy years and in 1944 the club mourned his loss. So did many other organizations in Victoria and the local morning paper honoured his passing with an editorial which concluded an impressive list of his public services with the simple words "This was a man."

Charlie Tapping, on the other hand, faithful purser of the Thermopylae Club for over ten years never went to sea — except once!

But he does know a lot about the old ships, this the fruit of the years between 1898 to 1904 when his work in the London offices of George Duncan and Company, shipping agents and ship owners, took him on hundreds of visits to the London docks in the time when sailing ships still made up a good part of the vessels tying up there.

These visits furnished Charles Tapping, always possessed of an observant eye and retentive memory, with a wide acquaintance with the wind-ships, and today when there is some question as to the rig or fate of some old-timer the memory of this 83-year-old man is often useful.

Only fifteen when he first donned the bowler hat and stiff collar demanded of even the most junior member of an office staff in those far-off days, by his second year he had been promoted to shipping clerk, a position which took him often to the docks.

How glamorous he found them! Here were exotic cargoes that hinted at a strange East . . . elephant tusks eight or nine feet long, carpets fresh from the Orient dripping little piles of sand, or even camel droppings. Warehouses filled with strange scents . . . the malodorous asafedista, ambergris, civet, dragon's blood, and also some intriguing objects that looked like small monkeys yet were actually made up of aloes that held the mould of the skins in which they had been poured to dry.

As shipping clerk too at the salary of fifteen shillings a week this youth had the duty of cashing company checks for sums of from one hundred to three hundred pounds, and then still alone and unprotected, conveying the weighty bag of coins from Lombard Street to the Board of Trade offices in London's tough dockland, there to attend a superintendent from the Board of Trade and a master mariner in paying off the crew of the latter's ship.

In his last year at the office he read the telegram that made him probably the first man in London to know that the canoe *Tilikum* was nearing Britain. The information came from the master of a vessel that had called at Plymouth shortly after speaking to the

68

Duncan Company's barque *Colonial Empire*. From the barque's master came the information that he had recently met, and succoured, the navigator and one crew-man of a very small boat who claimed that this unlikely craft had already sailed over 25,000 miles from Victoria, British Columbia via Australia. Since the captain seemed to feel somewhat dubious of the genuineness of this claim Tapping too dismissed the telegram from his mind, not to recall it till nearly thirty years later when he saw in Victoria the (at that time rathered battered) remains of the canoe *Tilikum*, a craft whose historic value had then not achieved the appreciation and publicity now widely accorded it.

The reason Tapping himself, though so intrigued by the life of the docks never went to sea, is explained in the following story.

"SHANGHAIED"

by C. W. TAPPING

In 1900 I was shipping clerk with George Duncan and Company of 2 East India Avenue, London E.C. This firm, besides owning the Empire Sailing Ship Line, were also ship and insurance agents for several firms, mostly Scottish, whose ships sometimes came into the Port of London or, as it was always called by "real" sailors, the London River.

In my position as shipping clerk I had to attend to entering and clearing the ships that came in at Custom House in Lower Thames Street, see to the financial end of paying off the crew and, in a general way, act as factotum to the captains.

In connection with my duties for one of these, the *Glenshee*, a small ship of 895 tons, I had the experience that gives its title to this yarn.

The beginning came when I had lunch on board the *Glenshee* after the signing on of the crew. Sometimes captains would take clerks to a meal at the famous Charlie Brown's Pub or the Railway Tavern in the West India Dock Road, but a lunch on a vessel in a saloon panelled with mahogany was the greatest thrill.

Waited on by the captain's steward and addressed as "Sir," listening to talk of foreign ports, I felt that this was the life of all lives I should like . . . and I said so. I said, "How beautiful it must be to look up at the billowing sails" — though at the same time forgetting that when the sails billowed the seas around were not of the mill-pond quality of those in the dock basin!

The officers solemnly agreed with my romantic pictures.

Next day the *Glenshee* was towed down the river en route to Cardiff for a load of coal for Cape Town. But — "back at the office" it was found that the captain had left behind the ship's papers. On the desk was the big linen envelope containing the Ship's Manifest, crew list and other vital papers.

These must be put in the captain's hands without delay so, as I was told, it was my duty as shipping clerk to draw money out of the petty cash and take the train to Deal, Sussex where the *Glenshee* would lay off in the Downs and drop the pilot. I was to get to the ship, deliver the papers, obtain a receipt for them and return to London.

It turned out to be more of an adventure than I had reckoned on!

To board the ship, there was first the climb by rope ladder to her deck, then on into the captain's cabin where I found dinner just commencing. At the table were the captain, two mates and the pilot.

The captain welcomed my arrival with the papers saying, "I had saved his life," etc., etc. He also invited me to join them at dinner, silencing my mention of boatman waiting beside the ship to row me back by saying I could return with the pilot.

I readily agreed.

At dinner there was a bottle of Bass' Ale for each diner, including myself. Up till now my drinking had been confined to a glass or two of wine but now I finished my bottle with the rest. I also ate a very generous dinner.

After dinner the men talked as they smoked their cigars. I listened ... I got very sleepy ... I started to nod. The captain said, "Lie down for a bit on my settee. I will call you when the pilot is ready to leave."

Two hours later I awoke. . . . The ship was moving under sail!

In great panic I spoke to the first person I saw, the steward. I said I was due back in London.

"Oh Lor!" he said, "we forgot all about you. But they can't stop the ship now. We've got a favourable breeze. You'll have to stay on board till we reach Cardiff" ... words that were repeated by the captain when, later, I poured my sad story in his ear.

Well, here was I on a ship sailing down Channel ... and I might as well try and enjoy it. BUT ... the *Glenshee* was in ballast, riding light, and she was also, as I found out afterwards, a "cranky" ship. And I had had a big dinner!

Let us not go too deeply into the consequences, except to say that when asked to take an interest in notable places along the coast, all I said was that I wanted to DIE.

Toward the end of my two and a half day voyage I did feel a little better but still, when we landed at Cardiff and the captain, as we parted at the railway station, said, "Well, son, do you still think a sailor's life is lovely?" I shook my head.

So ended my sea-going, the *Glenshee* my only ship . . . until the Thermopylae!

THE OCEAN

by JOHN AUGUSTUS SHEA

"Yes! where are the cities
Of Thebes and of Tyre
Swept from the nations
Like sparks from the fire;
The glory of Athens,
The splendor of Rome,
Dissolved — and forever —
Like dew in thy foam.

But thou art almighty —
Eternal — sublime —
Unweakened — unwasted —
Twin brother of time!"

IN THE GALLEY

IN THE YEARS from 1932 to 1966 the galley of the ship Thermopylae Club has had but two incumbents — Fred Kemp who joined on her very first voyage and Fred Jones who signed on in 1949. Yet on that first night how little did Jones dream, when he saw the dignified and solidly-built Kemp receiving all the respect due a charter member of the club, that this was once the lanky boy who, forty years earlier, had been lowly jo-boy in the steerage galley of the *Omrah,* the same ship on which Jones then filled the more prestigious position of cook — and in the second-class passenger galley at that! Not until some months later when Kemp gave his talk on the trials of a jo-boy's life was the coincidence revealed.

Other parallels marked the lives of the two destined to meet once more on the other side of the world. They were born in the same year (1881), both came from families sea-going for generations, neither was much encouraged by parents to carry on family tradition. In fact, if Fred Kemp's family had had its way, they would not have met at all. Their Fred was to be a naval architect, they said, but when, by the time he was thirteen he had three times run away to try to go to sea, they gave up, and in 1895 Fred Kemp was afloat.

For Fred Jones it was not until January 1900 that he left his home in Stepney, London, to join the S.S. *London City* as assistant steward. But Fred found the north Atlantic cold and stormy. Soon he transferred to the Royal Mail steam packet *Derwent,* operating in the inter-island trade of the Caribbean. An idyllic time that Fred now recalls with a rather wicked grin, and one during which he picked up the knowledge of cooking that was to lead to the galley of the *Omrah.*

73

Without relating all that befell the two Freds between 1902 and 1949, it may be noted that 1910 was a year of change for both.

For Jones it was the year he returned to sea after a lengthy time ashore, a move that was to lead later to his being among those who searched for survivors of the sinking of the *Titanic*.

Well does Fred Jones remember that night! At 11:15 p.m. came the astounding news that on her maiden voyage the unsinkable *Titanic* was sinking. First reaction on the *Mount Temple* was one of complete and utter disbelief. Someone in the cook's cabin even threw a boot at the wireless man who had disturbed his sleep with such ridiculous news! But when they found their vessel changing course to help in the search for survivors they realized it was all too tragically true.

At the end of that voyage, when Jones came ashore at St. John's it was to leave the sea forever. But not to forget it, as his faithful attendance at Thermopylae meetings shows.

For Fred Kemp 1910 was the year when, at home on the Isle of Wight between voyages, he met a Victoria lawyer visiting the island on his honeymoon. From him the seaman heard fabulous stories of the opportunities on the Pacific coast, and hither he came.

For the first few years, still a care-free young bachelor, he worked around this coast in summer and in winter returned to his native isle.

Then came the war of 1914 and Fred returned to Great Britain and joined in the dangerous work of mine-sweeping in the North Sea.

Soon after the war he married, became father of a son and decided to return to British Columbia. In 1920 he went ahead to prepare a home there, but when Mrs. Kemp and Jack did follow, the journey to the Queen Charlotte Islands was marred by the sinking of the ship on which were all their possessions. After a few years they moved to Victoria and settled in the quiet Cadboro Bay district. But their adventures were not yet over for in the summer of 1932 while the three of them were on a boating picnic they became the first to see the fabulous monster now affectionately known as "Caddy"!

Now Fred Kemp is no more, and it is the stentorian voice of the other Fred that rings out when Eight Bells is struck to open the new Dog Watch: "Eight bells, Sir. All's well and the lights are shining bright."

The story that follows comes from Fred's Kemp's bachelor days.

74

ON THE NORAH, IN THE CHARLOTTES, 1910

by FRED KEMP

In the year 1910, in the month of January, I boarded the G.T.P. steamer *Prince Albert*, ex *Bruno*, at Prince Rupert. The weather was wretched, a strong S.E. blowing, the rain streaming down, which after a heavy snow had converted everything to slush.

We had a rough passage across Hecate Straits, and punched against a strong southeaster round Rose Spit. Our next stop was Skidegate, then Queen Charlotte City, then on to Pacofi, my destination. Pacofi was situated at the head of Selwyn Inlet on Moresby Island. The letters P.A.C.O.F.I. stood for Pacific Coast Fisheries.

Upon arrival our troubles began. We found the head of the wharf intact but between that and the shore end it had collapsed. Teredos had eaten the piling. An awful looking gangway had been replaced across it temporarily.

A mixed crew took our lines; white, Indians, Chinese and Japanese.

I gave my letter of introduction to the manager who informed me I was to combine the job of skippering the small steam tug *Norah*, with looking after the nets and general work around the plant. This consisted of a large cold storage, fertilizing plant and oilery.

There was about six feet of snow over everything, so it was some mess. The trawler *Kingsway* was the only boat fishing at that time, but the last trip out she had been iced up and was now lying alongside waiting for milder weather. A terrible stench pervaded everything. It appears the company had been in liquidation, freezing the small shareholders out, but in the process they had been thawing the fish in cold storage. The compressors had been stopped for days on end, with the consequence that the large quantities of salmon, halibut, and mixed fish, had partially thawed out.

Then the juice had been turned on full blast, and as a result everything was frozen in a solid mass. They were trying to pry this apart with peevees, but all to no purpose, so it had to be thawed out again and used as fertilizer.

What a mess it was! About 400 tons lying on the dock waiting to go up in the elevator. Rotten and decayed fish everywhere.

Wading through the mess, I followed the manager along a half-of-a-plank sidewalk to the bunkhouse and dining room. Believe me, that sidewalk took some navigating! It was about eighteen inches wide and, across some of the gullies, it was eighty feet to the rocks below. Besides this, the whole surface was covered with lumps of snow. The bunkhouses had been built that far away on account of the stench from the plant.

Finally the crew arrived for supper, quarrelsome and discontented because their overdue wages had not arrived on the boat, as they had expected.

The next day we started to overhaul the *Norah*. The chap who was to be my engineer soon found that the water had been left on in the boiler, tubes had frozen and burst, and we had to send to Vancouver for new ones.

The rains had now started, and night and day, day and night, it was one continuous downpour. Oilskins were useless — you were soon soaked to the skin. There were about sixty of us and we had no drying room. Imagine the clothes of all those men festooned everywhere. The whole place was like a thick fog.

Everyone was working outside at the time, cutting trees for piling, repairing the wharf, and general overhaul.

I did what I could to the tug, then took a couple of Japanese into the net loft, where we fitted out a herring drag, seine and some gill nets. We were working in the warm and dry and were the envy of the poor fellows outside.

The weary winter wore away, and we made preparations for the herring. About the end of March I took the tug, scows and seine boats and went through the Lagoon Inlet to the head of Cumshewa Narrows. We arrived late in the afternoon and there was so sign of herring. We anchored at the head of the inlet to wait for morning.

When we turned in (I had a bunk in the wheelhouse) there was a fresh breeze blowing up in the inlet, and the lap of the small seas against the side was very distinct, but when I woke up in the morning though the wind was just as strong as ever, the water seemed a flat calm.

On investigating, I found that the herring had arrived. The whole surface was covered with oil. What a sight it was, millions of herring all working towards the shoal water to spawn. The males had already commenced to shoot their milt, and the whole sea was like thick cream.

From the air they were preyed on by every sort of bird. The eagles would dive right into the water and come up every time with one or two in their talons, and from the sea, they were attacked by dogfish and small sharks. It was nature in the raw.

I had the dinghy lowered and, taking a small gill net, I shot it out over the stern. The water was so clouded that the fish went into the net at once, and it commenced to sink with the weight of fish. We then got busy with the drag seine and at every shoot it was chock-a-block. We brought the scows alongside and salted them down as they came aboard. We made three trips. I do not remember the total weight but we got a good many tons.

Those fish were used mostly as bait for the halibut fishermen, and others were made into kippers. The amount of fish we made into fertilizer that spring was enormous, mostly edible fish; salmon, cod, halibut and flats of all kinds.

Later in the spring the whole Skidegate tribe came to Pacofi. The Indians fished for halibut off the Skedans Islands, and every day I would tow them to the banks and bring in their catch at night. In addition, we had a fleet of gas boats owned by Japanese and white men fishing halibut, two or three schooners, and the trawler *Kingsway* bringing in mixed fish. The latter used the otter trawls.

Towards the end of the summer we went after the salmon, mostly humps and dogs (pinks and chum).

We had a clam cannery about seventy miles down the coast near Jedway. It had not been running for a year or two, so I took the tug, a few whites and Paul Kato, the Japanese boss, who was a wizard with carpenter's tools. He was to supervise the repairs.

Passing between Lyle Island and the mainland, close to the Hot Springs, we came upon quantities of crude oil floating on the surface and found it in one place welling up from the bottom like a huge spring. It extended for miles on the water. (Author's note, 1966 —

77

Extensive exploration by American oil companies is currently being carried out in this area.)

Upon arrival at Bag Harbour we found the cannery literally overgrown, black bears around like dogs, and the whole harbour full of sea trout.

Paul Kato said that Mr. Ikeda, who has a copper mine in Ikeda Bay, had a small seine, so I took the *Norah* and ran down to see him. They were building the wireless station at Ikeda Point at that time, but it was a failure and they had to move it to Dead Tree Point.

Mr. Ikeda received us with Oriental courtesy, gave us a good lunch, and the loan of his net to return at our convenience.

We stopped for the night at Jedway, visiting Mr. Metcalf at the Jedway Hotel. The islands were full of prospectors, timber cruisers, and the hotel was full to overflowing.

In due course we fixed the cannery, and the Indian clam-diggers commenced work, so we upped stick and made for home. It was a beautiful day and as we came to Dana Inlet that night there was a full moon, but round it small white clouds were forming and then disappearing. I did not like the look of the weather and was glad when we tied up.

I slept that night in the bunkhouse and was awakened about five o'clock by the roar of the wind as it tore from the sea right up the inlet. By the time I had roused the engineer it was blowing a hurricane, and as we came out of the bunkhouse, it was all you could do to stand.

We started along the sidewalk, sometimes on our hands and knees. The roar of the wind was by that time appalling. Then all around forest giants began to crash. The sidewalk ran at this point right through the bush. The trees crashed ahead and behind, cutting the sidewalk to pieces. How we escaped was a miracle. Finally we crawled down a gully to the rocks to get to the plant. This was an undertaking made doubly difficult by the drenching, flying spray.

Blinded with sand we at last got into the clearing, and what a sight met us! Two large scows had broken from their moorings and were pounding on the rocks. Gas boats, row boats, were piled together in utter confusion. Finally we got to the lee of the powerhouse, the roof of which was gone. The engineer of the plant and a fireman and Paul Kato and a few Japanese were there.

Paul was wringing his hands and crying for the new scow he

had built on speculation; he saw himself ruined. He was taken seriously ill that night and, I believe, died in Vancouver.

We could do nothing but dodge the flying debris, but gradually I pulled myself along the wharf. By this time it was eight o'clock but it was still dim. My concern was the *Norah*. The head of the wharf was T-shaped and as she was on the lee side she was riding it out like an old shoe. Fortunately the piling was close and broke the violence of wind and sea.

I crouched for some time in the lee of the freight shed. Then there was a bit of a lull and I got back to the power house. The engineer had a tin of coffee, so we got a forge going and made a hot drink and made a bit of a meal.

Finally the wind abated and we surveyed the wreck.

Hardly a roof was left, everything movable had moved. A lot we never found again. Finally we got back to the bunkhouse by water. They were all very anxious about us. They were more sheltered and the roof stayed on, but a large tree had fallen across the centre of the house occupied by the Japanese. The father was sleeping at one end, his family at the other, but when they got them out they were not scratched.

We were weeks clearing up the wreckage.

GUARDIANS OF THE SEA

As GUARDIANS OF MEMORIES of the sea, the Thermopylae Club has undertaken a variety of projects. Of these most valuable was its part in the preservation and restoration of the famous *Tilikum*, the craft (basically an Indian canoe), in which in 1901 Captain J. C. Voss set out from Victoria, and three years and 40,000 miles later reached England after a voyage that took him across three great oceans and circumnavigated the world.

That this boat should, after all the admiration heaped on her at Earls Court, by the mid 1920's have become a derelict hulk, rotting in the mud on the banks of the Thames, seems today unbelievable. Equally surprising is it to learn that although in 1930 the efforts of the Victoria and Island Publicity Bureau and the generosity of the Furness Withy Line saw the canoe returned to its home port, the repair the hull was given was but rudimentary and it was left roof-less, exposed both to the weather and to the depredations of vandals.

So she lay for some years, but then there came one evening to the Thermopylae Club meeting some naval yachtsmen who had just sailed across the Pacific. These told the club members in no un-certain terms their opinion of a group that called itself ship-lovers yet neglected such a priceless, irreplaceable craft as the *Tilikum*.

The club sprang into action. Led by the dynamic Captain Mc-Donald, they soon collected the money needed to finance restoration and Captain Victor Jacobsen started on the work that saw her returned to, more or less, the condition in which she appears in the Maritime Museum today.

Later the Thermopylae Club, on the suggestion of old sealing captain Max Lohbrunner, and through the work of shipmate Bob

Dallaway (and with the permission of the provincial government) installed in her three hollow masts. These, though shorter than the original, do give some idea of her rig and also provide ventilation for the interior.

The club has also painted her hull and encouraged her removal to the protected position in Thunderbird Park that she occupied for many years. Today they rejoice that now she, like themselves, enjoys the hospitality of the Maritime Museum in Bastion Square, Victoria.

Another spot that finds *Tilikum* and Thermopylae close neighbours is on the Causeway wall above Victoria's Inner Harbour. Here 28 bronze plaques make up the Centennial Parade of Ships which commemorates vessels that had some historic connection with Victoria, *Tilikum* and *Thermopylae* of course among them. The first was donated by the Royal Victoria Yacht Club, the second, presented by its namesake, is easily found since it is the only tablet bearing an illustration of the craft it memorializes — a non-conformity not achieved without effort and obduracy on the part of the veteran mariners!

Another reminder that Victoria was once the home port of this famous ship was the ten-foot water-line model of her entered in the History section of the Victoria Day Centennial street parade of 1958.

Built on the premises of the 100-year ship chandling firm owned by Shipmate Emerson Smith, and not far from the rings on the cliff at which the original clipper once tied up, the model is one of fine detail. That these are accurate was assured by the daily visits of Captain Harry Bilton to the premises on Wharf Street. It was by then 65 years since he had trodden her decks but he had not forgotten, although it is to be doubted that on so small a replica her figurehead of King Leonidas would be provided with the demountable sword whose removal, for safety's sake, the old captain remembered as one of his last duties before the start of each voyage.

Later this model was given to the Rainbow Sea Cadets in whose headquarters in Victoria West she holds an honoured place.

Yet a few miles farther west, above a little cove in Esquimalt Harbour, a concrete pillar marks the spot where, as the bronze tablet on it records:

"When Vancouver Island was an infant colony nearly a century ago it was here that the gallant sailing ships from the old world stopped to replenish their supplies of water."

Conceived by Shipmate John Keziere and carried out through the co-operation of provincial government departments, the generosity of city building supply firms and the sweat of sundry Thermopylae Club members, the cairn recalls the days when, from ships anchored off in Limekiln Cove, sailors poled to shore the floats loaded with barrels in which they would take on from the fresh-flowing stream water for the long journey back to Europe.

Today the sailing ships and most of the men who sailed them are gone, but through this publication of some of their experiences, it is hoped some little contribution may be made to the preservation and dissemination of the memories of those sturdy times.

CAPTAIN VICTOR JACOBSEN

CAPTAIN VICTOR JACOBSEN. The name was once universally known in the Pacific northwest where he was among the most intrepid of the sealers. It still deserves remembrance today as that of the man who restored the historic canoe *Tilikum* from a derelict hull to the condition (almost) in which she stands today in the Maritime Museum of British Columbia in Bastion Square, Victoria.

What made Victor Jacobsen the choice as craftsman when it was decided by the Thermopylae Club that the honour of the sea and sailors demanded that the canoe should no longer lie in the neglected condition in which it had mouldered for ten years?

First, the skill possessed by the man who, in youth, had trained for three years in a shipyard in Helsinfors; second, the fact that he had been familiar with Voss and his boat when, in 1901, the venturesome navigator was preparing *Tilikum* for the voyage that was to make maritime history.

It was a friendship easy to understand. Both had come from northwestern Europe — Voss from Germany, Jacobsen from the little town of Botney, Finland — both had an appetite for adventure and danger.

Jacobsen met both very early in his sea-going career. Signed on to a vessel possessed of one of those hard-case officers who figured so often in old sea stories he had not been many days at sea when he became the unhappy eye-witness of this man's brutal attack on another with a belaying pin. This was a fatal onslaught which ended with the victim's body being toppled, rapidly and unceremoniously, over the gunwale.

That the young witness lived to reach the next port is surprising. That the murderer then quickly disappeared is not.

In 1881 came Victor's last voyage round the Horn from Europe, this one a long 165 days on the *City of Quebec* as ship's carpenter. On arrival in Victoria he found that men of his trade were earning a princely five dollars a day on shore. So who shall blame a young man who had left a mother in Finland struggling to bring up a fatherless family, for "jumping ship"?

Knowing that a description of himself would be given to the police, young Jacobsen made for the thick forests covering the sides of Mount Douglas, five miles north of the city. Here clothed only in work shirt and pants, he spent two foodless days, repairing at times to the mountain's summit from which he could watch for the departure of the *Quebec* from the harbour.

At last she was gone and the hungry youth could emerge from the forest. Nearby, fortunately, he came upon a farm whose hospitable owners not only fed him the most delectable newly-baked bread he had ever tasted, but also provided him with work and a bed.

Here he laboured till the activities of beavers flooded the farm, and sent him to the city.

This was a time when the sealing industry was just beginning to show signs of the riches it was to yield. Jacobsen was in at the start. First out past Flattery in the crew of Captain William Spring's *Favorite* (first schooner to be built near Victoria for sealing), then as mate on the *Mary Ellen*, first Victoria schooner to reach the fabulous hunting grounds in the Bering Sea.

But working for others was not good enough for a man as vigorous and enterprising as Jacobsen. He must have a boat of his own. With little money to spend, his first craft, the damaged 23-ton *Mountain Chief*, needed a good deal of repairing before she was ready to go to sea. Even then, by the time they reached the north, water from undiscovered leaks had destroyed much of the salt planned to go between the layers of skin. (Luckily he was able to get more from other sealers.)

To get a hull he could trust, he must build his own, an idea encourged by the girl with whom he was planning marriage. On November 10, 1888 he took two big steps. He married Minnie McLean and he laid down the keel of the schooner *Minnie*. The ship was to be seventy feet long, have a twenty-foot beam and draw seven feet. By May of the following year she was ready to go north.

He set off in high hopes on his staunch new vessel, determined before his return to have enough to pay off what was left of the debt incurred in building her.

But by now sealing in the Bering Sea was not as simple as it had been. Governments were intervening, revenue cutters were active in seizing vessels operating, or said to be operating, in prohibited waters.

It was the U.S. cutter *Rush* which met the new *Minnie*, took possession of her pelts and spears, put an officer on board, and ordered her to the nearest port.

But a captain so recently a bridegroom and new ship-owner was not to be easily defeated!

Exaggerating the discontent which his Indian crew was feeling after the last season (during which so many of their race had been left to reach distant homes in small hunting canoes) Victor Jacobsen convinced the revenue officer that if the *Minnie* were not allowed her freedom, he would not be answerable for the consequences.

Enough said! Hunting was resumed with such spears as the revenue man had not discovered, the boarding officer reputedly helping in the hunt! By the time the *Minnie* arrived off Nitinat there were 950 seal skins and nine sea-otter pelts between the layers of salt in the hold.

At Nitinat, just beyond the entrance of the Juan de Fuca Strait that led to home, Jacobsen found that his troubles were not yet over. Revenue vessels were patrolling the straits, ready to seize any boat carrying skins.

Now Jacobsen's longtime comradeship with the Indians (he was said to be the most consistent employer of Indian crews) came into service and enabled him to go silently by canoe in close to the Vancouver Island coast to the San Juan River. Here he engaged large canoes to which the pelts could be transferred and brought to Victoria. They sold for enough to pay off the Indian crew, settle the debt on the *Minnie* ... and leave Jacobsen with $35 in his pocket!

He had only one regret. He had not known how valuable were the sea-otter skins, until one of his sold for $3,000. He could have taken many more!

Though the *Minnie* served him well, in the end she fell victim to the rocks of the Unimak Pass far west in the Aleutians. Jacobsen himself was, at the time, confined to his bunk with an infected eye. This later had to be removed.

Other boats followed, most notable the *Casco*, once owned by Robert Louis Stevenson.

Last of all was the *Distributor*, a Skeena River passenger boat. Anchored in West Bay, Victoria, not far from the big house Victor had built in 1892, she became the unconventional home of the Jacobsen family for twenty years.

From her, in the summer of 1937, the old Finlander used to go each day to carry out the work on the canoe, *Tilikum*, for which the Thermopylae Club had provided the funds. Spinning oakum for the repair was octogenarian Jacobsen's grand-daughter, Marie, daughter of Captain E. H. Sweeney, superintendent of Vancouver Island pilots.

This work finished, Jacobsen had still a good few years to live. Not till he was over ninety did the Finlander, who had so long ago watched from the summit of Mount Douglas for the departure of the *City of Quebec*, "up anchor" for the last time.

SEALING . . . HISTORY
AND TREATIES

*In the Archives of the Thermopylae Club are several stories left by
the sealers of long ago. Among today's crew are three men who have
personal memories of those exciting, dangerous and profitable days.
To add to an understanding of the stories and men the following
history of the era of seal-hunting is given for those unfamiliar with
the subject.*

PRACTICALLY THE WHOLE HISTORY of fur sealing in the north
Pacific lies within a short quarter century — that incredible period
between 1884 and 1911, when the men of the Pacific coast, exhibit-
ing an amazing mixture of enterprise, courage and perseverance
went forth against the herds of seals, that had from time unknown
bred and died in the North Pacific. . . . Within this short span they
reduced a species that numbered millions to less than 200,000
animals.

Seal-hunting had, of course, been known in the Pacific before
1884. Even in 1800 the odd skipper from Boston had joined with
Russian crews on this ocean, but until after 1880 almost the only
sealing done in the north Pacific was by Indians, and these took
only the small numbers necessary to supply themselves with food
and clothing.

During the 1850's some few men from Victoria did hunt along
the west coast and in 1868 one attempted to stimulate the Indians
to increase their catches for trade. Still it was not till 1881 that the
first schooners specifically planned for sealing went out around
Cape Flattery and even down to the mouth of the Columbia River
in search of the animal whose pelt sold so profitably.

The men who manned these vessels soon noted that the seals had a fixed route, regularly approaching from the south and continuing north, though at a rate too fast for the schooners to keep up with them. At first they sought to increase their catches by going farther south, gradually working down to the coast of California. One ambitious captain who took his vessel to the Galapagos Islands returned with a single skin — and that taken off Crescent City, California!

Then, around 1882, came the word from a schooner prospecting for metals along the Alaskan coast and adjacent islands, that in the Bering Sea were seals innumerable. Later they were to find that the islands in this sea were the breeding grounds on which the herds of the North Pacific gathered annually.

In 1883 the American schooner, *City of San Diego*, with a white captain and Indian crew, became the first New World vessel to hunt in these rich grounds.

The next year the *Mary Ellen* of Victoria was there too, her crew whites. In 1885 she went again with the same crew, accompanied by the Sooke-built schooner, *Favorite*, carrying an Indian crew. The plan was to try to find which men, Indian or white, made the more successful hunters. Results were so close as to prove nothing but with the combined catch of the two vessels (around 2,400 skins) selling for $35,000, the race was on.

The next year 200 canoes and 500 Indians were carried to the Bering grounds by sixteen schooners. Six years later the mother-ships had grown to one hundred and twenty-two!

Some of these were built in Victoria, or elsewhere on the southern part of Vancouver Island. Others came from the Maritimes by way of the Horn. The *Pathfinder* was the first to make the long journey, a profitable experiment for her importer, since in her first season she took 2,000 skins.

As in ever-increasing numbers the schooners ranged the north-west Pacific, the supply of skins on the market grew — and prices dropped. This greatly incensed the Alaska Commercial Company which had a twenty-year lease on the Pribiloff Islands, main breeding grounds.

This group appealed to the American government which reacted by declaring the Bering Sea no longer "international," but "enclosed" waters and therefore under American jurisdiction. Under this ruling one legislator even went so far as to call seals "domestic animals"!

American naval boats now began patrolling these waters, schooners were seized, some more than seventy miles from land, and much litigation ensued. Russia saved the day by reminding the Americans that when they (the Russians) had owned Alaska, and had tried the same tactics, the Americans had waged a successful legal battle against them.

To clear up the situation a treaty was signed at the Tribunal of Paris in 1891. Under this, hunting of fur seals was prohibited within sixty miles of the Pribilof Islands, while in the Bering Sea generally it was agreed that seals were to be killed with spears only. (Seals sink quickly after being wounded or killed and those shot by guns were more likely to be lost and wasted.)

Both British and American vessels patrolled the sea to enforce this treaty, but with clauses sometimes reviewed after the schooners had left for the north, officers of revenue cutters would often find the captains of ships boarded ignorant of (or claiming so to be) the rules now in force.

In the early 1890's vessels were often seized. Captains and mates were imprisoned (one captain lost his mind after the supposed disgrace of this) and Indian crews were left with only small hunting-canoes in which to make their way to homes hundreds of miles distant. Much suffering, both mental and physical, followed — and some deaths.

To escape the surveillance of the revenue cutters, the larger schooners now began to make the long journey to the Japanese coast, off which were islands where the seal also bred. Within a few years these seals too were almost wiped out ... though not before the Japanese had become alerted to the wealth that lay in the ocean, and awaited their boats too. (In 1893, of the 70,000 skins brought into Victoria 29,000 came from Japanese waters.)

From then on sealing became the object of more and more re-strictions, restrictions, be it noted, that the Japanese, who had not signed the Paris Treaty, had no obligation to observe. By 1911 it became evident to all that the golden years were over, and that there was no hope of improvement except by full agreement among all nations hunting in those waters.

In that year Japan joined Britain (still signing for Canada), Russia and the United States in signing the International Pelagic Sealing Treaty, by which they all agreed that for the next fifteen years the Bering Sea was to be closed to all pelagic hunting. The only exception was for the original inhabitants of the region, who might hunt as their fathers did, with spear and canoe.

At the end of the period agreed on, the treaty was to be renegotiated at 12-monthly intervals. It remains in force today. Though under it pelagic hunting was prohibited, a certain number of fur seals was still allowed to be taken on land. By the Americans, on the Pribilof Islands, by the Russians on the Commander Islands in the Sea of Okhotsk, and on Robbens Island in the West Bering Sea. Of these skins, the treaty directed, fifteen per cent was to be given each year by each country to Canada, and an equal amount to Japan.

(Recent reports in the daily press record the sale in January 1966 in Montreal of Canada's share of the 1965 furs — 5,818 skins that sold for $621,241, but it should be noted that this was the gross taking, and on a year of fine skins.)

So, suddenly fifty-five years ago, hundreds of men in Victoria lost their means of livelihood, and for those who were boat-owners there was the added blow of finding their schooners saleable at only a fraction of their former value, if indeed a buyer could be found at all.

They appealed to the government for compensation but were refused. This reply led to recourse to legal advisers but the results were still negative. So in argument and privation ended the golden quarter-century of sealing. Today, save for the imposing house built by the renowned and daring Captain Victor Jacobsen, little remains to tell of the days of the sealing fleet.

THREE WHO WENT NORTH

THERMOPYLAE "shipmates" Maxie Lohbrunner, Frank Fredette and "Tab" Ross (later Captain A. E. Ross of the B.C.C.S.S.) who sailed in the sealing schooners over half a century ago still clearly remember those strenuous days.

Frank, for instance, remembers so well the build of the small hunting boats carried on the decks of the schooners till the herds were reached that not too long ago he built a faithful replica of those efficient little "shells" that were designed to travel easily through rough water and to approach their prey quietly. (The plans for this he sent to the Smithsonian Institute to fill a gap he had noticed in its book, "Early American Small Boats.")

This summer the three sealers of seventy years past gathered at Frank Fredette's summer home and, in the sheltered waters of Deep Cove, took in Frank's boat the positions they once occupied when afloat on the frigid, foggy waters of the North Pacific.

In those days each sealing schooner would carry eight such boats. When the hunting grounds were reached, these would be launched and fan out in a circle, roughly fifteen miles in diameter, around the mother ship. Soon, whether by rowing or by spritsail, each would be hunting alone, the other boats lost to sight in the heavy swell though sometimes glimpsed faintly as a triangle of sail on the horizon.

On each boat were the day's provisions, a small keg of water, a bundle of hard tack, bully beef, perhaps a pie — Captain Ross relishes the memory of the prune pie produced by the cook of Victor Jacobsen's *Eva Marie*, the schooner on which both he and Frank went north. Young Frank, however, was not then able to go in the

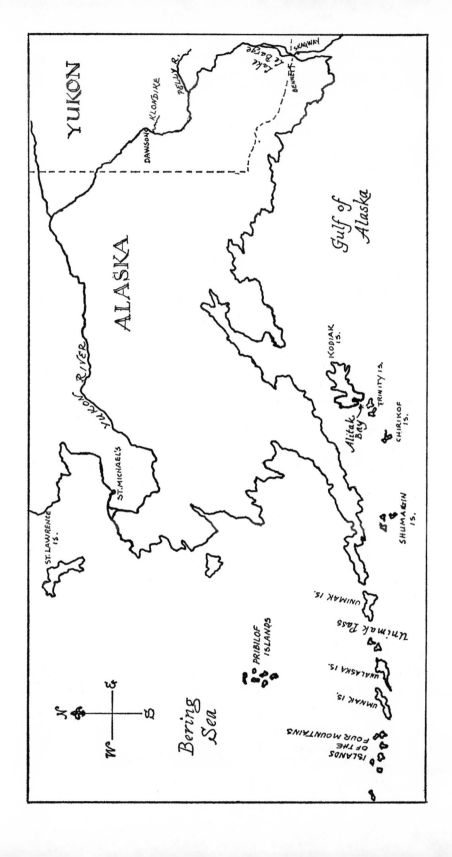

boats, for his job was that of cabin boy, the one crew member who, with the captain, remained on the schooner when the hunters went out.

Some vessels carried white men, some Indians. In the case of the white hunters, there were three to a boat, the "steerer" in the stern, facing forward, usually on his feet as he pushed rather than pulled on his oars. When the seal was sighted his was the responsibility to get the boat into the best position for the kill. Amidships was the "puller" who would know by the steerer's signals for silence when the seal was near. In the bow, the "hunter," key man to the prosperity of all, but especially so for himself.

He worked under a sliding scale that was decidedly stimulating. For up to fifty seals in one season, the hunter received two dollars per head. Over fifty and up to a hundred, the price for all rose to three dollars. A catch of over a hundred would give him four dollars a head for the season. Renowned hunters such as Maxie Lohbrunner, were known to be offered even more.

The steerer and the puller, on the other hand, besides a wage of fifteen dollars a month, also received seventy-five cents per head for each seal brought in by their boat.

Some schooners carried Indian canoes and crews. In that case 25 slender hunting canoes might be carried by one vessel. At the sealing grounds each canoe would set out with an Indian hunter; with him, to paddle and steer the canoe, his wife.

Though all hunting in the Bering Sea after the Tribunal of Paris was supposed to be by spear, it is not to be thought that men with the audacity to face the tremendous dangers of northern seas would be too precise in their observation of regulations, and so among the ropes at the foot of the mast was sometimes one that, when the revenue man came near, led over the side to guns trailing below.

Seals the old timers divided into three classes: "travellers," who raced through the water, often jumping from wave to wave; "moochers," slow movers who only occasionally raised their heads for a look around; and, lastly, "sleepers" who lay peacefully on their backs, some with flippers crossed on breasts, others with one little wing lowered below for balance.

Any sentimental thought raised in the reader by this defenceless scene was certainly quenched in the heart of those in the boat., whose only interest now was in getting as close as possible before the sleeping animal should awake. If he did, they knew his first act would be to put his ears below the surface to determine the direction of the sound that had disturbed him, his second to dive and make off.

Swiftly then up with gun or spear. Fire. Out with the gaff, and hurry to retrieve the wounded or dead animal before it sank. Or perhaps it might only be stunned, and the gaff must be hooked under the flipper and the little beast raised with great caution, "Sometimes it would take us ten minutes to get it up."

Once in the boat the teeth of a seal only wounded could be sharp and strong. "One bit my knee right through my sea-boots," recalls Captain Ross.

In general the seals were taken back to the schooner unskinned. In fact up to six made a good ballast, but on lucky days of heavier catch some would have to be skinned then and there. Wherever it was done care had to be taken to leave a layer of blubber on the inner side so that the layers of salt that separated the pelts during the months in the hold should not touch and burn it.

Sealing held many dangers. Worst were the fogs that abounded in those waters, fogs that would separate hunting boats from parent ship, and take them out of earshot of the guiding guns fired from the schooner, or out of sight of the flaring oily rags put up at the mast head. Then for the crews that never came back — and there were many — there came the moment when the last of the hard tack was gone, the water keg empty, and the cold growing worse.

There were stories too of boats cut in two by killer whales in this hostile world where the eerie red glare of volcano could add to the wildness of their surroundings.

But for those who did get back, life on sealing schooners is remembered as happy. Once the day's kill had been skinned, and the results entered in the log complete with details of place where caught and sex, there was a good supper. Food was varied though salt beef (this came in 200-pound barrels) and beans were indeed the backbone of their diet. After supper, gambling, and talking, occupied the evenings.

Despite all the butchering, sealing schooners are remembered as clean ships. Clothes were washed by trailing astern, and chances to have a steam bath were seized on whenever they reached a beach where a fire could be lit. Here in some abandoned cabin, stones would be heated and then water thrown over them.

But at last would come October or November. The breeding

94

season over, the seals scattered, and it was time for the hunters to leave the Bering Sea or Japanese coast and sail home. Some rejoicing in a catch of over two thousand, some with but a few hundred.

But after 1911 all this ended. The men had to seek other work, and in the course of time the desolate and useless schooners disappeared from the harbour of Victoria in which they were, for a time, a sad reminder of the days of fortune in the north.

TOPSAIL SHANTY
(tune — Blow the Man Down)

ANONYMOUS

As I was walking down Broughton Street
I went into Speedie's my shipmates to meet.

The crowd was all there, pretty tough-looking crew,
To have our peasoup and salt horse to chew.

The Old Man is tough and a hard-looking guy,
To get more than your whack is no use to try.

The duff is like rubber and heavy as lead,
With roaches in plenty for raisins instead.

The cook is a soaker who loves a good booze,
Twixt him and the steward there is little to choose.

And talk of the Bosun, he is tougher than tough,
In handling poor sailors he is much more than rough.

Supercargo is stingy and with stores he is mean,
On robbing poor sailors he is awfully keen.

I don't like to sail in this rotten old tub,
With no grog allowed and the poorest of grub.

When we get to port I am leaving the sea,
I'll get work on land and a farmer I'll be.

And now I have come to the end of my lay
For the topsail's aloft and the Mate said, "Belay!"

CAPTAIN DAN BUTLER

ANOTHER SEAMAN from the Atlantic who, like Kinney, chose the Pacific for his latter years was Captain Dan Butler, the widely and affectionately known "Captain Dan." Unlike Kinney, Butler's service as a sailor included fresh-water-borne craft as well as salt, and by the time he joined the first Thermopylae Club meeting of November 1932 his experiences were as wide as Canada.

Even before his teens this Newfoundland boy was at sea with his father — off to the Banks or with the Atlantic sealers. He had also been on one voyage to Hudson's Bay on the survey ship *Alert*. On this voyage he had met grim evidence of what a sea-going life could mean when, at desolate Marble Island, he had seen nineteen seamen's graves, men who had never got home.

Soon after this Dan Butler moved on, first to the vessels of the Great Lakes, then to British Columbia. Here he joined the men who went north after seals but unfortunately the only yarn he left of this era is extracts from the logs of other sealers.

Next prospect to tempt the Newfoundlander was the Klondyke Gold Rush of 1898. (see stories on pages 123 and 129).

With the close of the Gold Rush, Captain Dan, now a married man, returned to Victoria. Here, in co-operation with the Brackman-Ker Milling Company, he built two vessels, the *Forager* and the *Grainer*. These were used to carry from the Fraser River Valley farms, hay and grain to the company in Victoria.

In 1917 he returned from retirement to work for a time as rigger at the Wallace Shipyards. Then retirement again.

With the 1930's he welcomed the formation of the Thermopylae Club with its opportunities to talk with other old salts. He was one of its most prolific spinners of yarns.

FROM LOGS OF SEALERS
OF THE 1890'S

by CAPTAIN DAN BUTLER

THE SUCCESS OF a fur-sealing trip depends largely on the hunters, and they, to a certain extent, depend on the pullers, the greater part of whom were first-class boatmen and good sailormen. But there was another type, as the following extracts from old logs show.

The master of the *C. D. Rand* cleared for sea early in 1897 and the first entry in his log reads: "Noon, January 20, 1897, Lat. 40° 25′N., Long. 125°W. G.... R.... has this day refused duty by refusing to go in his boat when ordered to do so. John O. Townsend, Master: G. R. Ferry, Mate."

R.... reply to the charge was that he could not work on the food he was getting. Six other boatmen had the same excuse, but Captain Townsend was no weakling, for the next entry in his log book reads: "From noon Jan. 20 until 8 a.m. January 24 these men have been on bread and water. At 8 a.m. this day they told me they were willing to go to work, so I ordered the cook to give them the usual provisions that they were getting before they refused duty, and they resumed their duties."

Usually the food on a sealer was good. An extract from the log of Captain Baker reads: "At sea on board the *Pioneer*, April 2, 1897, Lat. 43:17N., Long. 125:05W. Seaman McC.... came aft and said the food was hard. What did you have for supper? I asked him. The barley soup was good, and there was salt beef and potatoes, tomatoes, onions and roast mutton and there was hot rolls, peaches, prunes, coffee, butter, milk and sugar, but this food don't agree with me and I don't get enough when pulling boat. W. E. Baker, Master."

Another extract: "Killa(?) May, March 12, 1903, Lat. 49:8N., Long. 126:52W., J.... refused duty. He would not go on deck

97

and work and keep his watch saying he would do no more work on this schooner. Again at 2 a.m. on March 13 he was asked to take his watch but refused. 6 a.m. on same date, he said again he would do no more work. I ran into Friendly Cove on the 16th of March and paid him off. Ologan (?), Master."

Aretis' log reads: "Hakodate, Japan, July 27, 1896. W. H. . . . , when put on board by the police, refused to go below and when ordered to work refused. 'I will not work. I will swim ashore. I will never work on this schooner.'

"Same date: This is to certify that P. T. . . . was put on board, and at the Consul's request, in irons. He refused to work in such words as, 'I will never do a stroke of work on this schooner,' but Captain Martin had a greater will-power than they, and he soon had them working."

The next entry in his log reads: "At sea, September 30, 1896. I do hereby disrate P. T. . . . on account of his not being able to steer. I have sent him from the wheel three times and furthermore, he is one of the most obstinate men I have ever seen. P. Martin, Master."

Log of *Pioneer* reads: "May 25th, 4 p.m., Lat. 51:20N., Long. 171:10W., W. H. . . . at the wheel, vessel under double-reef foresail, storm trysail and stern staysail, wind W by S blowing a heavy gale with high and dangerous sea running. Mate on watch. Vessel pitching heavy in head sea. H. . . . was sitting on wheel box and leaning against the wind. Mate told him to stand up and ease the vessel in the head sea. H. . . . replied, 'She is all right. I can steer well enough this way.' Mate said, "Are you going to stand up?" H. . . . then replied, 'No, I am not.' Mate at once called me and asked me if I allowed the man to keep the position he was in at the wheel. I replied, 'Certainly not,' and told H. . . . to stand up and steer properly. He said he would stand at the wheel as he liked. I told him to do as he was told. He at once left the wheel and told me that if I could steer her any better to take her myself and said, 'You have been chewing long enough,' and took off his mittens, threw them on the deck and put himself in a threatening attitude to fight.

"I told him I would log him and went below to do so. W. E. Baker, Master. D. J. Butler, Mate."

Log was read to H. . . . His reply to question, what had he to say, is what he said was for the mate who is always making trouble. He denies that he said to the mate, "If you want any fancy talk I will give it to you when we get in." When the mate said the above statement was true, he said, "Don't talk to me, I would not believe you on oath." He further said to me, "You can log me if you like. I guess I can make it as hot for you as you can for me." To the mate he said, "I did not alter my position from the time you told me till the Captain came on deck and I did not move after he told me, either." I asked him if he moved when he left the wheel and told me to take it. He said, "I have moved since."

In answer to if it was me or the mate he wanted to fight, "I did not want to fight anyone."

H.... went forward and told the men that I had written in the log that I intended making it hot for all hands forward. Men came aft in a body to see what I meant. I showed them the log and they found there was nothing of the sort recorded there. Michael Connell spoke for the men.

NOT ALL SEALERS CAME BACK

by CAPTAIN OSCAR SCARF

ON THE 31st of March, 1886 I shipped as boat puller on the sealing schooner *Pathfinder* with my two friends, John Charters, hunter, and Shortie Hinds, boat puller. We went south as far as San Francisco, hunted north and returned to Victoria on March 17th, St. Patrick's Day.

I did not like the job and went back to my ranch at Otter Point. My place in the schooner was taken by Wm. Blyth of Victoria.

About two weeks after leaving on this trip, on one hunting day, the boat containing Charters and his two men did not come back to the ship and, after looking for them for several days, the schooner went on to Ucluelet on the west coast, sending to Victoria for another boat and crew to replace them.

Ed Sheilds, a brother-in-law of Charters, and Mr. Andrew Bechtel, owner of the schooner, came to Otter Point and asked me to take my friend Charters' place as a hunter, until (they hoped) he could join the schooner again.

I left Victoria with my boat and two men with Captain Douglas Warren on the steamer schooner *Dolphin,* and joined the *Pathfinder* on the west coast. We spent the summer in Bering Sea. When we came south again we learned John Charters and his two men had not returned, and no trace of them has ever been found.

In the early spring of 1890, I left Victoria on the sealing schooner *Viva* and joined the *Pathfinder* (her name then changed to *Pioneer* for the second time), on the west coast. We were due at Shumagin Islands in the Aleutians on the 25th of June to meet the steam schooner *Mischief,* which had been chartered to take stores to the sealing fleet, and bring the entire Spring catch of furs to Victoria.

About the 20th of June we were off Kodiak Island in a heavy

gale and drifting before it. The captain thought we had plenty of room, but the next day he called all hands on deck. On going up, I saw that Chirikof Island was close on the starboard side with the surf breaking over it.

Our only chance was to get the ship around, and we passed the N.E. point of the island just outside the surf.

Captain Morgan decided to go to Alitak Bay, some forty miles away, but the chart showed some sunken rocks in the way, so he then headed for Kodiak Island until daylight, when we should have a clear run in.

Just after daylight we were among the Trinity Rocks and it appeared impossible to avoid one about fifty feet from the ship's side. The *Pioneer* was at that moment given up for lost by all of us, but just then a wave like a mountain lifted the schooner like a cork and threw her over the rock. There was some damage to her ropes and sails, but no one was badly hurt.

Anyhow, the *Pioneer* was still afloat, although in the confusion no one knew whether she had hit the rock or not. Finally we ran her ashore in Alitak Bay. She did not have a scratch on her.

We went on our way again, met the *Mischief*, ran through Unimak Pass, in a gale of wind, and several days later found ourselves becalmed near the Burning Mountain on Bogosloff Island. With some of the hunters, I went near the island in one of our hunting boats. The rocks were covered with sea-lions which were making strange motions. We found out later they were picking up their ballast. All sea-lions are so fat that they cannot swim under water without extra weight, and carry from five to fifteen pounds of small stones in their stomach.

Some one shot at the ones we saw and so many came towards us that we thought they would sink our boat. However, instead they went under it, but we lost no time getting away from there.

We hunted in Bering Sea all summer and returned to Victoria with over 2,000 fur seals.

The *Pioneer* went out later with another captain and crew. She never returned. Victor Jacobsen said he saw her in Unimak Pass heading for home but she was never seen or heard of again.

About the same time the schooner *May Belle*, with a crew of Becher Bay Indians, my friend Ed Sheilds in command, left Victoria for the west coast. She did not arrive there, and no trace of her was ever found.

B.C. SEALERS . . . RESCUERS . . .

by BEN AXHORN

ONE YEAR I sailed in the *Mascot*, Captain Lorenz, with a crew of six and a Japanese cook. We were the first to leave that season as we were to carry Indian hunters and had to go to Masset, Queen Charlottes, to pick them up.

It was some time in February before we got our Indians settled aboard. We were taking six canoes, 12 men and a cook, 13 in all. The time to sail had come at last, and with a fair wind we started on our passage to the coast of Japan. The Indians assembled aft, and as we passed their Rancherie sang the hymn, "God be with you till we meet again." This was taken up by those on shore, their voices blending perfectly. It was something new in my experience. I thought it a good omen.

After a few days out, we visioned a good passage across, as we were running wing and wing day after day and getting down to good weather, when the unexpected happened. She sprung a leak!

It was decided to run for Honolulu, with the pump going night and day. The lower berths of the Indians became untenable, every roll washed the bottom of the bunks.

We made Honolulu one Saturday night, raining and blowing. I was on the lookout when the mate came along. "We are going to heave to. Let the jib run down and haul the fore staysail to windward."

I asked, "What is the trouble?"

He says, "The Indians heard someone calling for help."

We could hear nothing owing to being rigged in oilskins and sou'westers, and we doubted if the Indians had heard anything either. But sure enough, they had.

They lowered a canoe and two got into it and went out into the night to windward. They were gone quite a time and we began to wonder, when at last we heard them coming along. As they passed under our stern to lee, we saw they had got what they went for. They had picked up three Japanese fishermen whose boat had been capsized in one of the squalls.

Our cook being of their race, got in conversation with them, and found out that our vessel was their last hope and they thought we were going to pass them by. They got a good welcome from the cook. They did not seem to mind their water-logged condition. One of them piloted us to an anchorage, then the Indians took them ashore. The news soon spread. Sunday morning we towed her into dock with the boats and in the afternoon the Indians held a thanksgiving service. Moody and Sankey's hymns were sung, which interested quite a number of visitors on the dock.

Time was passing. It was now well into March and nothing to show for the owners, only expense, so I must take you a little farther on to show you how we balanced the budget.

Leaving Honolulu with lots of fruit on board, we ran into a regular trade-wind which carried us straight across and left us in a dead calm. We took a chance and lowered our boats, and found ourselves among the seal-herd. In three days we picked up nearly 500 skins, and I think, by the first of May, we had more skins than any sealer on the coast.

We had more than once changed the name of our schooner from *Mascot* to Jonah, but we took it all back. She was still a *Mascot*!

...AND RESCUED!

by BEN AXHORN

In 1891 I made my first trip as a sealer and stayed with it for six years. The sixth year I got a hint I had enough. In this way:

That year I was in the *Agnes Macdonald* hunting Indian fashion, that is to say, two to a boat, my brother and I being together. We got our boats to Yokohama, and fitted them up ready, each to his own ideas, and went out to sea to about 200 miles off Kinka-San.

It had been blowing hard, but by noon it had calmed down some, but still one of those long, oily swells running and a dirty look overhead. Captain Cutler was doubtful, but all hands were eager to go.

"All right. Lower away, port side inshore, starboard side off shore. Off we go."

The late Captain Will Bragg was mate and hunter, with two men in his boat (my brother and I), in the inshore crowd. We found no seal, and about dusk found us back aboard the vessel.

It began to breeze up, and was getting foggy, but still there was no sign of the offshore crowd. I had been with the mate before and he got restless and uneasy regarding the offshore boats. He asked me to go out in his boat, and see if we could signal them by shot-gun.

I went. And we never saw the schooner again for ten weeks.

We delayed too long starting back for the vessel, the weather getting worse and more of it. When we got to the position where we expected to find the vessel, we lowered our sail and listened for the gun, but the incessant roar of the sea drowned all other sound unless you were dead to leeward.

We ran off again and listened, but no gun, so we decided to lay to till daylight. Our prospects did not look very bright, so we made a drag (sea anchor) by lashing our sail and two pairs of oars together and made it fast to the boat's painter. We still had one pair of oars which we kept for backing astern after the combers broke on the drag.

Morning came but no vessel in sight; blowing harder than ever, the wind offshore. So we passed the day, keeping clear of the breaking sea. Night came and no change.

I was at the oars the morning of the second day, when the wind chopped round and began to blow just as hard inshore. We waited till daylight, hauled in our drag, put up the mast, set the jib and started for land, course West.

For a time, the wind against the sea made wet sailing. Then the sun came out to cheer us up. Next we reefed the mainsail and set it, travelling pretty fast till noon. We talked and wondered if we would find a safe landing place if the wind would hold.

Around 2 p.m. we saw the loom of the land, which gave us great hopes, but to get there by daylight was the question. Yes, give her the whole mainsail — and we travelled!

As it was getting dusk we could make out an open beach with lots of people there, I guess wondering what was coming. We still kept all sail on her.

When a big comber picked her up and rushed us in like an express-train, we looked at each other for we knew we were in the surf belt.

"Quick work. Lower the sail." We just got the mast down when we were off again, racing toward the shore, and we knew we were in for a bad time making the landing.

We took the halyards from the sails, and with the main sheet, made ourselves fast to the boat, not short up, one end on the boat, the other around us like a belt — and we were ready. I was at the oars. We were making quite a few speedy rushes, getting nearer to the shore, so what?

We were about 200 yards off shore when we were picked up by the stern and carried right over, landing bottom up. Neither of us was hurt, just rolling around in the surf.

It was now getting dark but we could see quite a commotion ashore, much running to and fro, then we saw a Japanese coming off to us, and then another, and another, until there was a long line of heads bobbing up and down in the surf. How they dodged it, going right through the combers and coming out the other side!

At last the first one reached the boat and, with the line they had carried out, made fast. Soon we felt ourselves being towed shoreward. When we picked ourselves up and were on our feet there was much cheering. We found ourselves the centre of a big crowd. No one could speak English, so we could only thank them by grabbing their hands and shaking them.

Then the police came and took us away in rickshaws to their quarters where we were stripped, rubbed down, given a kimono, a bowl of saki and some hot rice, and made comfortable. They did not know who we were, could not ask questions, and we were equally helpless. But they gave us the best they had. Who could do more?

A STRANGE FIND

by BEN AXHORN

IN 1889 when I was in Victoria on the Liverpool barque *Tythonus* and moored stern on by the Custom House, two schooners, the *Triumph* and the *Sapphire* were moored near. From the watchman we found out that they were sealers, and all about them. It interested me so much I thought one day I would come back and try it.

In 1891 I joined the *Mary Taylor*. This was a time when Victoria was the home port of about 60 schooners engaged in the sealing industry. The upper harbour and water-front presented a busy scene when they were getting ready for the voyage which provided work for 1,200 men.

In the year 1893 the fleet was prohibited from catching seals in the Bering Sea and both British and Americans were there to stop any vessel caught doing business. Still we went up there in the *Mary Taylor*.

The days were long and we had seen no cutters, until one morning, when we were on the feeding ground off the Pribilof Islands, smoke was seen on the horizon. Captain Petit was vexed as there were quite a few seal about, and we were looking for a good day's catch.

There was a good breeze at the time so we decided to give the cutter a run. All sail was set and, making a fair wind of it, we ran to the northeast, and, as if to help us elude the cutter, a thick fog shut down, and we changed our course to the northwest and so she missed us. We kept on till noon, when the fog cleared up and no cutter in sight.

Good! Lower the boats. Off we went, but we found very few

seals. We were too far north. One by one the boats found their way back to the schooner. All but one. Then we saw it quite a way ahead and stood towards her to pick her up. As we drew nearer we saw that the hunter was signalling, so we set our staysail to get to her quicker.

We hailed him, "What's the trouble?"

"No trouble, Good luck, I hope. I have found a dead Right whale."

We picked up the boat and in another hour we ran alongside, and moored stem and stern to the prize. Then, how to handle it was the problem.

"Unshackle the chain from the anchor. Get it around the head and heave away on the windlass. Then we can get at the jaws and the bone." We were working fast as it might breeze up any minute.

"All fast. Heave away!" But instead of lifting the head, the schooner was going over.

" 'Vast heaving. Make all fast. Well, if it won't come up to us, we got to go down and get what we can."

Among our crew were two old Salt Spring Island half-breeds who understood what was to be done, and it was a great sight to see them taking spells at sawing out the bone, sometimes under water, and passing it along.

With our primitive methods we got around 1,500 pounds of bone, from three to eight feet long, perhaps longer.

However, it began to breeze up and we, reluctantly, had to let go. Had a good clean up and lay round hoping for another fine spell, which did not come.

Two days later we fell in with a whaler and signalled her. Getting within hailing distance, our skipper told him about the whaling we had done and gave him the bearings to find it.

"I've been looking for that whale the past week," he said. He was very pleased, thanked us, and squared away for the position.

I hope he found it. It was a monster. You could walk on it away beyond the schooner's length fore and aft, and I would say it was three feet above our rail. When we were away from it, it looked like a small island covered with birds.

Back again at the sealing grounds, we got one good day's hunting, and picked up quite a few seals with the prospect of another day nearly dead calm, when again smoke appeared and we could not run this time.

It was the American cutter, *Corwin*. She lowered a boat and, on coming alongside said jokingly, "We got you this time, Cap."

The officers came on board, sealed up our guns, and we were ordered out of the Sea.

Under the circumstances our skipper did the best he could, took it with a smile and we headed for the Unimak Pass, on the way home to Victoria. We had a good run home, and what one could call a fair catch.

OCEAN

by ROBERT POLLOCK

Great Ocean! strongest of creation's sons,
Unconquerable, unreposed, untired,
That rolled the wild profound, eternal bass
In Nature's Anthem, and made music such
As pleased the ear of God! original
Unmarred, unfaded work of Deity.

SEALING SCHOONERS I REMEMBER

by CAPTAIN VICTOR JACOBSEN

A SCHOONER that had a very strange experience was the *Prescott*. At the time it happened she was operated by a crew which had brought her down from St. Michael's in the Yukon after the Klondyke Gold Rush. When her owner went broke, crew members Hargrave, Galine and Captain Lambrose seized her for wages and brought her from Seattle over to Victoria.

She was San Francisco-built, about 40 tons; very sharp, about six inches dead rise to the foot. She had lead ballast between the timbers and, this being valuable, the three men took it out, and replaced it with ordinary gravel.

Though both Galine and Lambrose had navigation papers and could take charge, it was decided that Lambrose should be Captain and Galine Mate. Hargrave was the sailor and a Frank Le Grand cook.

They fitted her out in 1902 for the sealing trade, and sailed down Barkley Sound to the Indian village at Dodger Cove where they picked up and signed on 17 Indians. In February they sailed out to the sealing grounds at the mouth of the Columbia River. These were the best sealing grounds at that time of year.

They had been working there for some time and had taken about 70 seals when a heavy southeaster sprung up. The schooner was hove to under reefed sails.

About midnight Lambrose had the watch on deck, with four Indians. Lambrose was not well acquainted with the coast and didn't know how these storms work, so when all at once it dropped dead calm, though there was a heavy sea rolling, he and the Indians shook the reefs out of the foresail. In a few minutes the wind chopped round to the southwest and struck the schooner heavily. With the sea running the other way, she turned over clean round, broke the mast and bulwarks and lost the four Indians and all the gear overboard. Three of the Indians got on board again, but one struck by some object from the ship, was killed.

The rest of the crew was asleep below and did not know what had happened. When the schooner turned over some water came in below and the crew rushed up on deck to find everything on the vessel swept away. They at once got buckets going, bailing out the water, but as she did not take any more they knew that the vessel's bottom was not damaged.

As luck happened, the Seattle-San Francisco steamer came along the same day and asked them what they wanted done. They wanted to be towed into some harbour but the mail steamer's captain said he couldn't do that and, instead, took them and the seal skins off the schooner. He then sent his carpenter to sink the damaged boat by boring holes.

This was the only vessel known to go clean around and all the crew saved.

GEORGE NICHOLSON

THAT Victor Jacobsen was not the only sealer to defy the authority of the patrol vessels is shown in the following story told by shipmate George Nicholson, otherwise known as Major George Nicholson, author of the popular book *Vancouver Island's West Coast — 1762-1962.*

Although not a bona fide career seaman, George Nicholson's 35 years on the west coast of this island where business and other duties took him often afloat make him a valuable member of the Thermopylae Club. Here he has held for the last two years the position of Supercargo.

Valuable too is the demonstration that he gives that even on the threshold of eighty years a man can still compile an absorbing book, and then go out and market more than six thousand copies of it.

Add to this activity his interest and help in establishing the identity of the remains of long-lost Fort Defiance, found recently beside a cove on Meares Island by his young friend, Ken Gibson of the west coast community of Tofino.

Site of this historic structure (built in 1791-1792 by the men of the American vessel *Columbia*, first ship flying the Stars and Stripes to circumnavigate the globe), had long been a matter of disagreement among those interested in the history of the Northwest Pacific coast. Today, thanks to Gibson and Nicholson, Meares Island is proved to be the spot.

CAPTAIN GEORGE HEATER, SEALER, DEFIED CAPTORS

by GEORGE NICHOLSON

THE WEST COAST OF Vancouver Island has produced hundreds of tales of sailors who fought gale, tide and fog in an endless quest for fortune. One of the greatest of them was George Heater, master of sealing ships. The following story tells of a brush with a Russian patrol during the height of the seal hunting era in the North Pacific.

At 11:45 p.m. on July 22, 1893 when proceeding under full sail in the western portion of the Bering Sea, the Victoria sealing schooner *Ainoko* was overhauled and ordered to stop by the Russian cruiser *Yakout*.

An armed boarding party came on board and her master, Captain George Heater, was charged with violating the terms of an agreement then in force between the British and Russian governments; that the Canadian vessel was hunting seals in a 30-mile wide zone in which all sealing was prohibited.

On behalf of his owners and the crew, and in vindication of his own position, Captain Heater protested the seizure and insisted that a record should be made in writing and given to him; claimed that the commander of the *Yakout* was aware that the *Ainoko* had been driven by heavy seas within what he described as "the limits." Also that it was impossible to pursue and hunt seals in such adverse weather.

Furthermore, that the commander of the Russian cruiser had full knowledge of the fact that the *Ainoko*, immediately prior to being overhauled and ordered to stop, was proceeding in full sail in an opposite direction from the prescribed waters, unaware of the proximity of the *Yakout*.

The Russian admitted that all the facts and statements made by

Heater were true but, since there was no British naval vessel near, he must order Captain Heater and the *Ainoko* to proceed to Yokohama, Japan, where he was to report to Her Britannic Majesty's naval consul.

Finding remonstrance in vain, Captain Heater headed for Yokohama. On board with him were three white men, a Chinese cook — and 23 Indian hunters and canoemen from Hesquiat on the west coast of Vancouver Island.

It was these Indians who changed Captain Heater's mind. Go to Japan they would not and so the captain had no alternative but to change course and head for Victoria. Paying the Indians off when he reached Hesquiat, he proceeded on to Victoria which he reached on August 28th.

Here Alexander Rowland Milne, Collector of Customs, had no choice but to seize the *Ainoko* and its cargo of skins. Heater followed this by lodging with him a ship's protest, and after a hearing before Mr. Justice Crease the vessel was released.

Another adventure of Heater's was when his command, the 120-ton schooner *Markland*, was caught in a sudden storm in the Bering Sea while all her Indian hunters were scattered across the horizon in their cockle-shell canoes. Only through Captain Heater's fine seamanship were they all picked up, although in the process the *Markland*'s upper structure was partially demolished and all canoes were washed overboard.

Despite the damage she finally reached Unalaska where repairs were made, canvas replaced, new canoes purchased.

Six weeks later she reached Victoria with a record 2,240 skins!

ELUDING THE RUSSIAN CRUISERS

by BEN AXHORN

CAPTAIN J. WHITELY and myself had been shipmates for quite a time, so when he took charge of the *Labrador* I just naturally went with him. Captain P. J. Hickey was mate.

In the early part of the season we dodged a few southeasters by running into Ucluelet but there came one we could not dodge. It was in March when we were off Cape Cook in company with the *Maggie Mac*, another sealer. We were pretty close inshore and, with a falling glass, too close in case of a bad blow. We ran off while the chance was good.

The expected came and we were soon hove to under a close-reefed fore-sail. Standing by the wheel was the mate who reverently made the sign of the Cross as the big combers came near us.

I remarked, "I wonder if the *Maggie Mac* came off shore?" His answer was that if she did not, her chances were very small. To my knowledge she was never seen again.

The programme was for the schooners to assemble at Port Etches, where the *Mischief* was to take the coast catch back to Victoria in July. Most of the fleet made it, but no *Mischief* put in an appearance. After waiting for a few days, it was decided that the *Labrador* should take the skins, which she did, though I did not go with her.

On the *Agnes Macdonald* there was a sick second mate. Captain Cutler came aboard the *Labrador*, and it was soon arranged for me to go with him as second mate, and the sick man to return on the *Labrador*.

I got my bag and was soon on my new schooner. Everything seemed so big after the *Labrador*, but after a chat with Mr. Sterling, the mate, I knew we should get along.

Soon we got under weigh and headed for Copper Island (Japan).

115

The run across took somewhere around fifteen days, sailing by the wind nearly the whole way.

I was getting to like my new berth more and more each day. You know, there is something in sail that makes a Liverpool pantile as succulent as Miss Fogarty's Christmas cake!

Finally there came a perfect sealing day, and by 5 a.m. all our boats were away. Even the mate had gone, leaving only the Captain, cook and myself aboard.

There was another sealer about two miles nearer shore. We made her out to be the *Vancouver Belle*. She too was under hunting rig. All seemed to be going fine.

At noon Captain Cutler took an observation and gave our position as 18 miles off the Island. Just then we noticed the *Vancouver Belle* hoisting her flag to call her boats home. We wondered why ... but not for long for soon we too saw smoke on the horizon. Soon our boats too were coming aboard, though it seemed to be a long time.

Meanwhile the *Zabraka*, a Russian cruiser, was getting nearer. The *Vancouver Belle* must have got all her boats aboard, for she was making sail though the cruiser was making for her and lowering a boat. The next thing we saw was the *Belle*'s head-sails run down.

We still had one boat out and two men at the masthead on the lookout for it. "There she is. Straight ahead, Sir." "Good! Just where we wanted to find her."

In three minutes at most we were off with every sail set, heading for our boat.

The cruiser had been watching us, for she was soon belching smoke from her funnels and heading for us.

We luffed for a moment to pick up our boat and then, with our flag still at the masthead, the chase began! It was kind of thrilling for as long as the breeze held the Russians could not gain on us. Our log showed from thirteen and a half to fourteen knots. In our flight we warned several of our schooners who also made sail and disappeared.

When darkness set in we changed our course and never saw any more of the cruiser.

I would like to mention a run we made the following year in the *Macdonald*. We were bound for Japan and eleven days out we were in a position beyond Honolulu. That would be good steamboat time in those days and, I think, for sail a record.

Charles F. Gray,
founder of the Cutty Sark Club,
Winnipeg, and Skipper of the
Thermopylae Club, 1950.

Major F. V. Longstaff,
prime mover in the formation of
the Thermopylae Club of Victoria.

Alexander McDonald,
San Francisco, 1897.

Captain Alexander McDonald,
Victoria, 1957. First Skipper
of the Thermopylae Club.

Lieutenant William Gregory, R.N.R., 1910. Now Captain William Gregory, member of the Honourable Company of Master Mariners and a Younger Brother of Trinity House.

Ship Senator, master C. P. Kinney, sailed from Puget Sound between 1904-1907 on three world voyages.

Captain C. P. Kinney (left) ashore at Shanghai sometime in the 1890's.

J. J. Moore, aged about 27.
Later mate on the Joliffe and finally
master of the Hydrographic Vessel
William J. Stewart.

The William Joliffe, one-time Liverpool tug, later British Columbia Coast Fisheries patrol vessel.

Charles Tapping (above) and Captain J. A. Philipsen (left), writers of the Log. The latter was also one of the founding fathers of the Club and the first Supercargo.

Captain George Kirkendale,
another founding father and the Club's
first Purser.

Captain Kirkendale (about 1910) in the office he occupied for 34 years as Shipping Master,
and later Port Warden and Harbour Master of the Port of Victoria. PHOTO COURTESY PROVINCIAL ARCHIVES

Captain Victor Jacobsen,
noted sealer and
schooner owner.

PHOTO COURTESY PROVINCIAL ARCHIVES

Captain J. C. Voss (seated),
skipper of the globe-girdling canoe Tilikum.
Photo taken in South Africa, 1903.

PHOTO COURTESY PROVINCIAL ARCHIVES

Captain Victor Jacobsen, over 80 years of age, at work on restoration
of Voss' Tilikum sponsored by the Thermopylae Club. PHOTO COURTESY PROVINCIAL ARCHIVES

Pathfinder, one of the first schooners brought from the Maritimes via the Horn specifically for sealing. PHOTO COURTESY PROVINCIAL ARCHIVES

A major tragedy in the history of the port of Victoria was the loss of the S.S. Pacific.

Steam tug Pilot took tows north to the Yukon, south to San Francisco. Note the half-roun planking used in construction of deck-houses.

Captain A. E. Ross,
boat-designer Frank
Fredette and Captain
"Maxie" Lohbrunner
check "Tab" Ross'
notebook for names
of the crews
they sealed with.

In the skiff designed by Frank Fredette; an exact replica of the hunting boats of the sealers.

Lieut.-Cdr. N. A. Beketov, R.C.N., once of the Imperial Russian Navy, later R.C.N. Senior Intelligence Officer, West Coast.

Captain G. A. Thomson, of the British Columbia Coast Steamship Service, on the bridge of the Princess Charlotte.

ABOVE: *Doyens of the Thermopylae Club: Cooks Fred Jones and Fred Kemp, J. B. White, Skipper in 1949, and Captain Harry Bilton, once apprentice on the Thermopylae herself. Bell was retrieved by Captain Frank Baylis from vessel sunk on the China Coast.*

BELOW: *J. B. White, Don Campbell and Fred Johnson make sure rigging on model of Thermopylae is exactly right.*   PHOTO COURTESY ANN WILSON

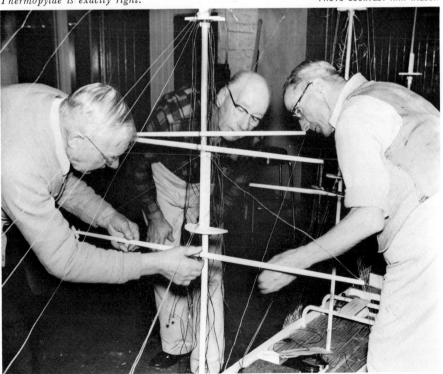

Ship Thermopylae on Bullen's Ways, Esquimalt, about 1893.
PHOTO COURTESY PROVINCIAL ARCHIVES

*oading 100-foot balks through hole cut in bow before Thermopylae sails from Puget Sound
or the last time, 1895.* PHOTO COURTESY PROVINCIAL ARCHIVES

*Ship Oronsay on
which C. F. Gray
was apprentice in
the 1890's.
Stormy scene off
the Horn painted
by her master
Captain Cook.*

Shipmates sometimes don fancy dress for annual Christmas banquet. Honoured guest at this one was John Guzzwell (back right), home from his single-handed world-girdling voyage in Trekka. ALSO IN PICTURE: *centre back, Fred Kemp; front row, left to right, Fred Johnson, Fred Jones, Frank Fredette and Bob Dallaway.*

SEALERS RUN THE BLOCKADE

by CAPTAIN OSCAR SCARF

IN THE YEAR 1891 there were many fine schooners on the coast with Victoria as their home port, including the fine schooner yachts *Vera* and *Casco*, also the *Molly Adams*, one-time speed queen of the United States fishing fleet.

Two of the finest were the schooners *Annie More* and the *Carmolite*, both owned by the late Captain Charles Hackett, a newcomer in the business, who raised the price of seals to the hunters from $1.50 to $3.25 per seal and got good crews of hunters for both his vessels.

At the time I shipped on the *Carmolite* along with the three Poirier brothers of Sooke. We hunted along the British Columbia and Alaska coast and about the 25th of June sailed into the fine harbour of Alitak on Kodiak Island to meet the steamer *Danube* which had stores for the sealing fleet. We put our skins on the *Danube* which was anchored outside the three-mile limit, but there were no stores on her for us, and we had to go to Sand Point for what we needed.

At Sand Point six or seven schooners were at anchor, but the *Carmolite* was becalmed about two miles from the anchorage. Captain Gardner, who at that time was mate of the *Annie E. Paint* and Al Bisset, came off in a rowboat and told us that all schooners at anchor had been warned not to enter the Bering Sea, and were getting ready to go home.

With Captain Cutler and another man, I went ashore in one of our boats. We were not seen by the coastguard. Captain Cutler sent me back to the schooner with orders to Charlie LeBlanc, the mate, to go to Squaw Harbor, some six miles away, and wait there till we heard from him.

Several days later Captain Cutler came out with our stores on the *Annie Paint*. We transferred them to the *Carmolite* outside the limit, and the schooners went on their way. The *Annie Paint* to Victoria and the *Carmolite* to try to run the blockade of British and American warships that we knew were all looking for us.

We sailed far out to sea with a strong gale and ran through the Kodiak Pass, about 1,000 miles further west, on the 4th of July, when we thought the warships would be in port for the holiday. We saw no ships and several days later hove to 100 miles south of the Pribilof Islands, where the weather was fine and seals plentiful. We took 1,600 fur seals in 16 days.

This, of course, was too good to last, and on the seventeenth day H.M.S. *Nymphe* from Esquimalt came alongside and her boarding officer told us to stop hunting and go home. He had sent the *Annie More* home the night before. We all put in big claims against the government for being stopped, but never got anything.

The *Carmolite* was seized by the Russians the next year, as was the *Vancouver Belle* and the *Rosie Olsen*.

In 1892 I shipped on the new schooner *Agnes Macdonald* of which I was part owner, a vessel carrying 1,800 yards of canvas and once making 307 miles in one day.

About the middle of June we sailed into Port Eleches in the Gulf of Alaska to meet the steamer *Coquitlam* which had stores for us. About twenty schooners and five warships were there and, while I was standing on the deck of the *Coquitlam* waiting for my mail, the United States cutter *Corwin* came alongside and after ordering us off the ship, towed the *Coquitlam* away. We never did get our mail!

Captain Bob Evans of the United States cruiser *Yorktown* came alongside the *Agnes* and told us not to enter the Bering Sea. There was nothing to do but go to the Russian coast. On the 18th of August the *Agnes Macdonald* in company with the *Belle* of Vancouver put hunting boats out 18 miles south of Bering Island. About 11 a.m. the Russian cruiser *Zabraka* fired at the *Belle* and put a prize crew on her. They also fired at the *Agnes* but the wind got up strong and the *Agnes* was soon making 12 knots towards Cape Flattery.

The Russians gave the crews of the vessels they had seized the small schooner *Rosie Olsen* to come home in. About 60 men came in the *Rosie*, the rest of them in different ways, some taking as long as two years to get home.

On one trip to Japan I met my childhood friend, Indian Jonnie, in Hakodate. I never saw Jonnie again after that. He was lost with most of the Becher Bay and Sooke Indians with the schooner *Sylvia Handy* the next year.

In 1897 I shipped on the *Agnes* again and went to Japan, but she lost her rudder 700 miles west of Honolulu and beat back with a jury rudder in 14 days.

The *Agnes Macdonald* went ashore in a dense fog at Nanariue Bay northeast of Japan on the 23rd of June, 1897, and we had to leave her. After being 16 days at Nanariue we were taken to Kiesa, 60 miles south, and put in jail, but this was because they had no other place to keep us in.

From there we went to Hakodate on the coast steamer *Jinjue Maru*. From there to Yokohama on the P. & O. liner *Otaro Marue*. and from Yokohama to Victoria on the C.P.R. *Empress of India*. Arrived here just in time to see the *Islander* steaming out of Victoria loaded with miners. The Yukon gold rush was on!

"RUSTY" CAMPBELL

ALTHOUGH TODAY stately in possession of legislature and university the city of Victoria once knew a much lustier time — a time when through it passed tens of thousands of men anxious to find fortune in the North.

Among those who viewed these north-bound transients was a certain "Rusty" Campbell, then but a boy, but later in manhood to do his own share of travel in the North.

For Rusty Campbell, however, travel in northern British Columbia was to be not in search of gold, but in the service of the Provincial Department of Forestry. Forty years he spent in this lonely work, before retiring to Victoria, city of his birth. Here, a bachelor, he found companionship in various clubs, among them the Thermopylae of which he was a member until his death in 1964.

Though not a seaman Rusty did have experience afloat to share when yarns were called for, his craft the canoe he so often used during his years in remote parts of the north.

A man with a wide interest in history and literature, he made the solitary life of the forest-ranger yield him rich rewards. To his inquiring mind, for instance, the finding that the Indians of the Interior spoke of Americans and Britons as "Boston men" and "King George" (the III?) opened speculation as to how these terms crossed the continent.

Most intriguing of all was the knowledge that the part of the province in which he worked was that across which the Scottish explorer, Alexander Mackenzie, passed on the historic journey that saw him the first white man to reach the Pacific coast "from Canada by land." And so, in 1914, the red-headed ranger, with a copy of Mackenzie's own diary as guide, undertook to retrace the course (in his area) of the century and a quarter old crossing — probably the first, and possibly still the only, man to have done it.

So precise was his duplication of the journey, that in writing of the crossing of the portage between the waters flowing into the Arctic Ocean and those into the Pacific, he says, "A.M. said it was 817 paces. I paced it. He was about right." Then he adds, "This place is still in the wilderness." (So was most of his "range"!)

Another never-to-be-forgotten, but more hurried, journey was the one undertaken by Rusty and three other young rangers in October of that same year when, emerging from a lengthy stay in the forests beyond Prince George, they found that their country had been at war for two months.

Delaying only to write up their reports, the four sped by canoe down the Fraser River to Quesnel and on again by land to the nearest recruiting station, fearful only that the fighting would be all over before they could lend a hand!

At the end of hostilities Rusty returned to many more years in the depths of British Columbia's north before retiring in the late 1950's.

He had hosts of stories but, unfortunately, the only one told at the Thermopylae Club that was left in writing is the fragment that follows.

Would that he might also have told the story of his father, the Reverend John Campbell, who officiated at the marriage of so many Victoria couples at his home, "Breadalbane," at the corner of Linden and Fort. This was the first house to be built on Linden Avenue which was, I believe, named by the Rev. Mr. Campbell.

VICTORIA AT THE TURN
OF THE CENTURY

by "RUSTY" CAMPBELL

For a while old Victoria, as I knew it, was in the turmoil of the Klondyke Gold Rush — ships loading with passengers and freight filled the wharves on old Wharf Street, just below today's Maritime Museum.

No dog strolling on the street was safe. Freight sheds on the waterfront resounded with yelps and barks of tethered dogs, all the way from little fox-hounds to collies. The only things these Argonauts forgot was dog-feed for the sleigh-dogs.

Ships like the old *Umatilla, Tees, Danube* and *Otter* left about weekly, complete with men, dogs and bottles, waved aloft by the big, brave (just then, at any rate) gold seekers.

It was also possible about this time for a curious boy to see the horsemen who had volunteered for the South African War being drilled in Beacon Hill Park.

Characters on the street were a boy's heroes. . . . Swift Water Bill Yates, famed river man of the Yukon, with his Viking blond moustaches. This was the sealer captain made famous by Jack London in the book *Sea Wolf*. There was also Klondyke Kate from the dance-halls of Dawson City and others from the Creeks.

There were actually streets of amusement for the men sojourning in the port. Dance halls and theatres like the old Savoy. None of these places was open, of course, to a boy, but we could look from the outside. Then there were the British Navy shore pickets, cutlasses and dress, salons galore. Another thrill came from visiting the ships that had rounded the Horn and seeing the cases full of muskets and cutlasses. We boys thought they were for repelling pirates.

FREIGHTING NORTH WITH
THE GOLD RUSH

by CAPTAIN DAN BUTLER

DURING THE Klondyke Rush of 1898 steamers were in great demand and, although nearly every craft that could be used was pressed into service, they could not accommodate all the eager gold seekers. The S.S. *Garoone, Pack Shan, Fastnet* and many others were used for the Alaska service, by our cousins across the line.

Old, worn-out craft were taken out of the boneyard, hastily repaired, a lick of paint and off they went. The *Santa Clare* was lost with some of her people, and others found the going very hard.

Conditions were a little better in British Columbia than across the line, but some of the craft that sailed away were short of all life-saving apparatus and boats, and most were overcrowded. My brother (Captain John Butler) had people sleeping on and under the cabin table.

In January 1898, I was given charge of the *Richard III*, an old dismantled barque formerly in the coal trade. The orders were to change her into a freight and passenger boat. A gang of men was engaged and bunks to accommodate about 70 passengers were built abaft the main hatch, in the tweendecks. While this work was going on, the tug *Lorne* towed us to Nanaimo where we took on about 500 tons of coal in the lower hold.

From there back to Victoria again, where we loaded machinery and foodstuffs. Oats, hay and other articles too numerous to mention came on too. In the foreward tweendeck we had horses and bullocks. On deck, owners found space for dogs. One owner tied his dogs to the anchor cable, forward of the windlass. He nearly lost them when we let go the anchor.

Next, men and women came on board till every bunk was filled, wives going with their husbands to face unknown dangers and hardships.

The tug *Lorne* had been engaged for $150 a day for the round trip, and early in February she took us in tow for Vancouver, where some 200,000 feet of lumber was put on the deck.

Often the old *Richard* had been got under way to the shanty of "Away Rio" and others. This time our departure was made to the barking of dogs and lowing of cows. The good old ship was drawing 19 feet aft, but it did not make much difference to the *Lorne*, at that time the most powerful tug on the Pacific, as up we sped through the Gulf and through Seymour Narrows.

Off Camp Point, near midnight, she circled very wide and struck an uncharted reef. The ship bumped and bumped and every time my heart bumped in unison, for it flashed through my mind, "Eighty souls on board. No life-saving gear and only one old boat."

The tugboat pulled and the strain on the hawser was terrific, but it held, and the ship was afloat again before the passengers reached the deck. There was quite a bit of excitement for a while, till it was made sure that the vessel did not leak.

We reached our first port, Wrangell, safely a few days later. Here some of our passengers left us for Dawson via the Stikine River. For two of them this was a tragic trip, for they quarrelled and one killed the other. By a strange coincidence, my brother took the murderer back to Nanaimo, where he met his fate.

During the last leg of our trip we had stormy weather with plenty of snow, and the dogs on deck got covered with snow and took sick. Their owners began to throw them overboard till I put a stop to it and made them shoot the dogs first. Then the distemper caught them all and they all had to be done away with.

Up the Lynn Canal we ran again into a heavy gale with intense cold, and our progress became slower and slower till, when off Henry Bay, it stopped entirely, so we had to go into this open anchorage to anchor. Here the old *Richard* began to bow to the rollers coming down the Lynn Canal, and here, day after day, the wind blew without a let-up, and our water ran short.

We signalled our tug, and Captain Langley left at once. The following day he was back with ice. It was too rough to come alongside, and never before had water been supplied in such a strange manner. The crew of the *Lorne* pelted us with lumps of ice till we had enough. Some of it melted at once and our cattle soon stopped mooing for water.

After a week's delay in Henry Bay we reached Skagway, a wide open little town with Soapy Smith one of its leading lights. Sounds of revelry could be heard every night from Chancey's dance-hall. I felt rather proud of the engineer's skill as a dancer. No one could hold a candle to him. His success, however, was due to his having slippers. All the rest of the dancers were shod for the White Pass Trail!

As soon as the horses were landed, they were at once set to work to haul freight along the trails. I was told they were earning $100 a day. The pack men got 25 cents per pound of freight from tide-water to the summit of the Pass.

I have often been to Skagway since that first visit when it was wild and woolly. When I got back to Victoria again I reported the reef we had found. The survey ship *Egeria* found that it came within 10 feet of the surface at low water. Quite recently a Japanese ship loaded with lumber came to grief on this same reef.

CAUGHT IN THE ICE
ON THE YUKON

by BEN AXHORN

THE 1899 season's work on the Yukon was drawing to a close and everyone who was going to spend the winter on the outside had gone, or were coming up with us on the *Nora*, the last boat of the season connecting with the lower river.

We were lying at the Bennett end of Miles Canyon waiting for the crews of the two boats that had been running all summer on the lower river, and whatever late passengers they had brought up to White Horse from Dawson. This was before the railway had got to White Horse, which meant a six-mile portage around the canyon.

We lay there for two days before the crews began to show up and, as it was getting colder, we were anxious to get going before the lake froze up.

Finally we were ready and, besides the two crews, had around thirty passengers. It was about noon when we got away and were soon steaming up the fifty-mile river but you can imagine our surprise when we got to the lake to find it one sheet of ice around two inches thick!

Having lots of experienced rivermen aboard, a conference was held and it was decided to try and force a passage through away from the shore line where the ice was not so thick. We kept it up for a time until long after nightfall. Captain Williams meanwhile watching down in the hold to see if she was making any water.

Suddenly he came rushing up. "Stop her. Get some sacks!" The ice had ploughed through her soft planks like a plane. In some places there was little plank left and she was making water fast.

We cut planks to fit between the timbers and, with a sack on the

126

side nearest the hull, nailed them fast. It was now decided to run back to the mouth of the river. We got there about daylight, and none too soon. She was down to the guards. Now to make a temporary ways.

All hands got to work. Four of the biggest trees were got, placed under her and we hove her out as far as possible, leaving the mooring line all fast.

Well, here we were a long way from Lake Bennett and no way of getting there only by Shank's mare.

A watchman was left in charge as we started off to navigate on foot over the ice. We left all together but we were soon a long straggling line, some wishing for skates, others bewailing their luck, — though the passengers never knew how near they came to not coming out at all and that we were very fortunate to be on top of the ice instead of under it.

That night we reached the Tagish Police Post, had a good supper of baked beans and rested till morning. Off again at daybreak, making Bennett that night. Next day we took the train for Skagway, forgetting all our little troubles now that we were homeward bound.

One should never get tired of a good thing, so the following Spring saw the same crew at Lake Bennett with two ship-carpenters and two truck-loads of supplies to repair the hull, walking back over the same trail.

The water had receded and left the *Nora* high and dry but she was full of ice and no way of getting it out only by chopping it. The damaged planks were first removed which gave us a chance to throw the ice out. It was a tough job but we persevered, and had her fixed, launched and ready for service before the season opened.

We cut a few cords of wood for the boilers and took her up to Cariboo Crossing at the bottom of Lake Bennett. The water on the crossing was too shallow to proceed further. Captain John Irving was there in his boat, the *Gleaner*, with a cargo of freight for Atlin but the shallow water that prevented us from getting up, also prevented him from coming down.

It was decided to put his freight on a scow which could navigate the crossing and we would take it on to Atlin. We did this several times till the rising water allowed the *Gleaner* to go through.

Work was about finished on the lakes, except for the Atlin trade and Captain Irving had that. Then word came for us to go to Miles Canyon and get ready to go through to the lower river.

Two out-riggers or platforms were built on the bow, two pilots with long sweeps were stationed there to help her round the many bends in the canyon.

Quite a crowd from White Horse lined the banks to watch the performance. "All ready. Let her Go!" Once started there was no turning back. We nearly brushed the side several times, but all's well that ends well. We did the canyon and White Horse Rapids without a mishap.

I put the summer in on the river and we came out in the Fall like princes in comparison to the previous year for we took the train from White Horse.

ON THE YUKON RIVER,
1898 - 1900

by CAPTAIN DAN BUTLER

DURING THE Gold Rush of 1898, Lakes Linderman and Bennett were places of great activity. It was on their shores the Argonauts built their boats for the 500-mile trip over lakes, rivers and rapids to the Klondyke. Soon the little town at the head of Lake Bennett grew into one of importance for, even before the railway (White Pass and Yukon) came, teams had been hauling planking, frames and machinery for the building of river steamers to the lake shore.

The steamers *Ora*, *Flora*, *Nora* and *Dora* were built and launched here. The *Gleaner*, belonging to Captain John Irving, and other boats, were built in this busy little port, and here also the steel frames and plates of the *Australia*, largest stern-wheeler on the upper Yukon were assembled.

All this fleet was employed carrying freight and passengers to Miles Canyon, returning each trip with the few that had struck it rich, and the many disheartened men who were glad to get away from an unkind land where toil and hardship brought them no reward.

In July 1900, I had charge of three scows loaded with cattle, bound for Dawson from the Cariboo. In Miles Canyon we stopped, unloaded the cattle and, with the help of the pilot stationed there, ran the empty scows through the five miles of swift current in twenty minutes. Next we tied up waiting to re-load the freight. The owner of the cattle and the herders arrived at last and, on counting heads, we found two horses and 74 steers, one of the latter having strayed on the trail.

The herders, about fifteen of them, searched through the night through the thinly-wooded country, but in vain. Next morning we re-loaded the cattle and away we drifted down the 50-mile stretch of river again to Lake Le Barge.

Here we hoisted our big square-sail and, followed by the other scows, away we went before a fair wind across the thirty miles of lake. During the night the wind increased and our deeply-laden scows made heavy weather of it, plunging and wallowing and going at a great rate.

Next morning we entered the narrow, swiftly-flowing river. It was my first trip down the Yukon, and I had been told to look out for the wrecked *Domville* around a bend. We found her partly submerged and our crew found it hard work to keep clear. A short while after, one of the scows piled up and we had to stop and come to the rescue. Back we had to walk upstream with ropes and blocks, and it took all our combined efforts to get her afloat again.

A few days later five small islands were sighted ahead. We took the right-hand channel around them, and rounding a bend, saw the steamer *Clifford Sifton* on the cable used by the up steamers in the swift waters. Our crew needed no urging to use every effort in avoiding striking the sharp stem of the steamer, for it meant all our lives. We missed the stem but crashed into her starboard bow, broke in our upper-works and went spinning round the next bend in the river just below. The other two scows followed our lead but passed without incident.

A little after this we sighted Rink Rapids and, keeping well to the right in order to avoid the sand bars, we drifted on.

Where the Pelly joins the Yukon there are many islands and sand bars. This place bears the sinister name of Hell's Gate. Running through we struck a snag and punched a hole in our scow. The cattle, when they heard the water running in, at once began to bellow. Fortunately we managed to beach on an island in time and here we landed our cargo, put a patch over the hole, and waited till morning.

We found the others waiting for us at Selkirk, one of the old Hudson's Bay fur-trading posts.

After being under weigh for fifteen days, and nearing our destination, we stopped one night at a police post across the river from Selwin. The following morning, before setting off, the crew struck, demanding more pay. Two weeks had gone by, and the lump sum we agreed on was considered not good enough. They told the owner that here they would stay, and the scows too, until their demands were met.

It was quite common to hear of strikes on the Yukon. It always brought visions of wealth to the gold-seekers, but ours was a different type of strike! Words passed back and forth, and when there were hints of damage to the outfit, I was told to get help from the opposite shore, and a limb of that great body known as the "Mounties" came back with me to hear the grievances of the crew. They were a mixed lot, Australians, Scandinavians and French Canadians.

The cattle owner from Hamburg told his story. He made a great oration, telling the mutineers he would get his scows towed the remainder of the way by the first steamer that came along. But he need not have worried. . . .

The men gave in after many hours delay and reboarded with their clothes. Soon after, we were under weigh again, and Dawson was reached two days later.

Here I said good-bye to my late companions and so finished our long drift down the Yukon.

CAPTAIN GEORGE KIRKENDALE

ONE OF THE Thermopylae Club's founding fathers who in youth had sailed from Victoria both north and south in search of fortune was Captain George Kirkendale.

An Ontarian of United Empire Loyalist stock his first choice of career had been that of teacher but by 1897 he had left the little school on Salt Spring Island to join the fishing fleet at the mouth of the Fraser. The next year he was off to the Yukon after gold. In 1902 he was after gold of a different kind — the pirate gold reputedly hidden on Cocos Island.

Although Kirkendale served on this voyage as a deck hand he already held a mate's ticket, and within a few years had also acquired captain's papers.

Very soon after this he gave up all the wandering and came ashore to the position that he held until his retirement 34 years later. Shipping master for the Port of Victoria was the first step; later came appointments as Port Warden and Harbour Master.

Always Captain Kirkendale was regarded as a very steady man, this stability of temperament being well-illustrated by the handwriting in every one of the more than 200 daily entries in his Cocos diary — regular and even whether in the humid climate of that tropical island, enduring at sea adverse winds and everlasting rain or abandoning at last the hope of fortune.

Crew on the brigantine *Blakeley* on this expedition were: 1st mate, Gus Whidden; 2nd mate, George Powell; starboard watch, Jim Easton, George Forbes and George Kirkendale; port watch, Shef Thompson, Gus Weirtze (?), and Jim Blackwood. Also a cook and three "instrument" men, of whom more later.

132

TO THE KLONDYKE
. . . AND BACK

by CAPTAIN GEORGE KIRKENDALE

IT WAS in the summer of 1897 that the big rush started. I was fishing on the Fraser River that summer when the news came through about the big strike, and I well remember the excitement among the fishing fleet at the time. Some of the fishermen quit fishing at once, went to Vancouver to outfit, loaded up their fishing boats, and away to Skagway.

Some of these fellows got through and did well, and I know I would rather trust myself to get to Skagway in a Columbia River fishing boat than in some of the floating coffins that went north with their gunwales awash with passengers and freight.

I made up my mind to have a try at the north, but I did not want to go over the Skagway Trail in the depth of winter, so after the fishing was done on the Fraser, with my partner Ben Stone, I came to Victoria and fished halibut and cod off Discovery and Chatham Islands for a couple of months.

In January 1898, we were ready to board the boat to go north. As I intended staying a year or more I had quite a heavy pack. I will give you a list of my outfit. One pair of Mackinaw pants, 2 pair overalls, 2 suits heavy underwear, one Mackinaw shirt, one cotton shirt, one pair leather boots, one pair gum boots, three pair woollen socks, one pair Arctic socks, one pair moosehide mocassins, one pair cowhide shoepacks with the hair still on, three blankets, a Stetson hat, some strips of blanket for nips to wrap around the feet inside the shoepacks, 2 pairs of mittens on a string, a piece of green cheesecloth, snowshoes, a rifle, a sheathknife, tin plate, cup and spoon.

If I remember it right we made Port Simpson (30 miles north of

Prince Rupert) in about two and a half days, then on into Wrangell by the following day.

(The next part of Kirkendale's tale covering his experiences in the North itself have already appeared in R. M. Patterson's book *Trail to the Interior* and may not be reproduced here. We next join the young man as the first signs of winter appear, at Telegraph Creek on the Stikine River.)

There I found one of my partners, George Fenn, who had gone up the river in our boat, so the two of us camped together to consider our next move.

There was a river steamer called the *Corsair* which had been tied up at Telegraph Creek for a month or so, and we heard that her owner, Captain Cooper, had come up to take her to Vancouver, and was looking for a crew. We applied and were taken on as no one else seemed to want the job.

There were only the Captain and an engineer and our two selves, but as we had the fireroom filled up with wood before we started, we reached Wrangell in a day. (Hence had no need to stop and cut firewood from the river bank for the engine-room, as was frequently the case.)

The Captain took the wheel most of the way down the river while we passed wood and fired boilers, cooked a meal, relieved the wheel in open spots, and otherwise made ourselves useful.

When we reached Wrangell I went up town to have a haircut and a shave (the first in nine months), and when I came back to the dock a few hours later I found that my partner was just pulling out on a stern-wheeler bound for St. Michael and the Yukon, escorted and helped by the tug *Mystery*.

Thus I missed putting in a winter frozen in the ice on the Yukon!

Now lying alongside the dock at Wrangell was Spratt's Ark waiting for a tow to Victoria. Spratt's Ark was a huge scow with engines and boilers, and twin propellors. With both engines going she could steam about three knots, but at that time one boiler was out of commission, so steam was kept on the other just to work the pumps to keep her afloat. She had been towed to Wrangell during the summer with 800 tons of coal aboard.

There were only two men aboard her, Captain Owen Thomas (generally known as Tommy Owens) and Harry Hornibrooke, the engineer. As I was acquainted with both of them, I took up my quarters on the Ark, and Tommy agreed to ship me as mate when we pulled out.

After I had joined her we lay there another two weeks. Then the steamer *Horsa* contracted to tow us south. We shipped two more men who agreed to work their passage to Victoria.

Spratt's Ark had the most famous siren whistle ever known on the coast. The only thing to equal it was the howling of the dogs in Fort Wrangell. The night the *Horsa* towed us out we turned the steam on and opened up our siren and ran the whole gamut of ten notes, up and down and up again. Everybody in Wrangell knew we were going, and the dogs took up the challenge and endeavoured to drown us out!

Although the *Horsa* was a big cargo and passenger steamer she was going south light, and found she could make only about three knots towing us. She took us as far as Port Simpson, ran us into the bay, told us to drop our hook, and then left us. We remained at anchor six weeks with absolutely nothing to do but eat and sleep and play poker.

After we had been in Simpson about a month the tug *Mystery* came back from St. Michael's. Shoo Fly Bill was the master, and Black Mike the engineer, and as Bill's wife was a Simpson woman, Bill had to stop and visit his relatives.

Harry and I were in Rudge's Hotel late that night when old Bill suddenly said, "Where's my goose?"

"What goose?" we said.

"My goose. The boys gave me a goose to take to Victoria, and some of you fellows have swiped it."

This was too good an opportunity. I slipped out of the hotel and searched around, and sure enough, I found a fine wild goose shoved under a bench outside. It did not take long to haul it out and chase down the wharf and drop it into our boat. I then got Harry and we put off to the Ark.

The *Mystery* pulled out for Victoria that night, and as two days later was Thanksgiving we had the regulation dinner of roast goose!

Two weeks afterwards the *Mystery* came back to Simpson to tow us down, and as soon as they came within hailing distance of the Ark, Shoo Fly Bill started shouting, "You stole my goose!"

We assured him we knew nothing about a goose, but unfortunately some of the feathers had got stuck around some of the timbers on deck, and Bill's sharp eyes soon picked them out. We never heard the last of that goose!

It took the *Mystery* two weeks to tow us to Victoria, as Bill worked the tides as much as possible, and we used to anchor every night and play poker.

We had a close call crossing Queen Charlotte Sound. A southeaster blew up before we got across to Christie Pass, and we were hardly holding our own, while the *Mystery* was rolling enough to throw her funnel overboard. I was at the wheel in the Ark. About two o'clock in the morning I roused out Harry, told him to shake up his fire on the one boiler, and get our little propellor going. It took him about half an hour to get sufficient steam to start up the engine. By that time we were drifting broadside on to the rocks a couple of hundred yards away but the little extra kick of our propellor just gave us enough headway to round the point and get into Christie Pass.

From then on without any further incident we made our way to Victoria, reaching there on the sixth of December.

So ended my year's outing on the Stikine and in Northern Cassiar.

PERHAPS FORTUNE LAY SOUTH?

WHILE, IN THE LATE 1800's, most Victorians seeking riches went
north, there were, betwen 1897 and 1902, four vessels which when
they passed Cape Flattery turned south in their search for fortune.
Their goal was the little island of Cocos, a few hundred miles west
of Panama.

Here was reputed to be concealed treasure beyond imagining.

First man to use the caves of Cocos as hiding place for pirate
loot was the naval captain, Edward Davis, who turned to this
nefarious profession in the late 1600's.

More than a century later another renegade, Captain Grahame
(later alias Benito) of H.M.S. *Devonshire* added another instalment.

Last substantial deposit arrived there on the British barkentine
Mary Dyer. On her had been loaded by authorities of church and
state in Lima the riches they sought to save when the liberator Boli-
var was feared to be approaching. The sight of such wealth was too
much for the British seamen and they absconded to Cocos.

That this last loot had indeed been hidden there was proved by
visits in 1844 and 1850 by the man Keating (sometimes written
Keyton) who brought away gold and jewels to the value of $35,000.
The other stories of concealment were probably equally true, the
hiding place each time supposed to be but temporary. But pirates'
led short lives and their secrets died with them.

To add to the difficulties of those who sought to recover the
treasure were the land-slides that obliterated clues and land-marks.

First Victoria group to join the many, past and present, lured by
the thought of this immense fortune, was that which left in the
Spring of 1897 on the 40-ton schooner *Aurora*. It was commanded
by Captain Fred Hackett, a brother of the Captain Thomas Hackett

who had received from a fellow Maritimer, Keating, the maps and papers that the latter had received directly from Thompson, lone survivor of the barkentine *Mary Dyer*. On the *Aurora* expedition was also Mrs. Brennan, former widow (third wife) of Keating.

Later that year another surprising vessel left Victoria and some weeks later turned up at Cocos. Officially, of course, the *Imperieuse*, flagship of the Pacific Station, and the accompanying *Amphion*, had gone south on a series of friendly calls on neighbouring nations but the presence on board of a certain C. Harford, disguised though he was as a newsman, later made this excuse rather thin! Harford was the man who had been brought to Victoria on the *Aurora*'s return voyage after the Victoria ship had found him there marooned when a Costa Rican gunboat had failed to return to pick him up.

When the naval vessels got to Cocos hundreds of blue-jackets were sent ashore to "dig for diamonds" — but unsuccessfully!

This little foray not unnaturally led to protests from the Costa Rican government, owner of the island!

The next year it was the later so famous Captain J. C. Voss who sailed for Cocos, but so well did he disguise his purpose that Victoria papers of the time report the setting out of the little 8-ton *Xora* as under the captaincy of Percy McCord and the "turn of the century" exhibition of Paris as her destination. Voss, in his *Venturesome Voyages*, speaks of her as a 10-ton boat and identifies himself (undoubtedly correctly) as captain. With Voss and McCord were young Harry Voss and a certain Haas (Hahn?).

A few months later they were back in Victoria, Voss ill from tropical fever and not a penny richer.

After this a pause until the autumn of 1901 when the Pacific Exploration and Development Company was formed in Victoria, its aim, the sale of 750 ten-dollar shares to raise the money to out-fit another expedition to Cocos. Captain was to be the experienced Fred Hackett and unusual angle of this undertaking was to be its use of some recently-invented "metal-diviners." These machines were said to be capable of locating gold and silver hidden underground from a distance of two hundred yards or more.

They were to be operated by Justin Gilbert, for many years Victoria court stenographer, and Daniel Enyeart of Washington, U.S.A. The two men, plus a Mr. Raub, went along on the *Blakeley* on its 1902 expedition as passengers. Among the crew members was George Kirkendale, extracts from whose diary of the voyage follow.

IN SEARCH OF PIRATE GOLD

by CAPTAIN GEORGE KIRKENDALE

ALTHOUGH Captain George Kirkendale did give a yarn to the Thermopylae Club, on December 13, 1933, telling of his experiences as a member of the crew of the brigantine *Blakeley* he left no written script with the club. The account below is made up of extracts from the diary he kept during the seven months of the expedition to Cocos Island.

*   *   *

DECEMBER 27, 1901: Shipped today on Brigantine *Blakeley* to hunt for treasure on Cocos Island. Spent the whole day shovelling ballast into the hold.

DECEMBER 28: As there are no stores on board lunched at the Queen's Hotel (Owned by Captain Voss who himself had gone to Cocos in 1897).

JANUARY 1, 1902: Took some of my friends down to inspect the *Blakeley* and from there to the W.C.T.U. Mission reception.

JANUARY 6, MONDAY: We hauled the ship to the end of the wharf where the tug *Mystery* (the same that had helped bring him from the north in 1898), took hold of us. Crowds of friends and interested spectators assembled . . . to bid us farewell and a lucky voyage, and many a joke and laugh was passed on the object of our expedition . . . they all have a sneaking idea . . . they had better invest in a share. . . . As soon as we had passed the Outer Wharf we caught a strong fair wind so we got all square sails on her and helped the tug. About 3 p.m. the *Mystery* dropped us well clear of Race Rocks.

JANUARY 7: At Flattery met heavy S.W. wind and sea. Turned and anchored in Port San Juan; forced to leave as anchor dragging.

Hove up the anchor . . . set sail and stood out for Flattery Light, so we were disappointed in our night's rest. All through the night it was . . . shifting and we had a steady drill at setting and taking in sail, slacking away and bracing up until we were completely fagged out.

JANUARY 8: Making eight knots.

JANUARY 9: . . . half a gale with a heavy sea running . . . when suddenly she took such a dip that she threw nearly everybody out of their bunks . . . shouts of "Clew up the foresail. Haul down the jib. Drop the mainsail." I looked into the galley and the first thing I noticed was the cook's boots adrift in a sea of molasses. A whole cask had capsized. . . . Pots, pans and broken crockery, bits of stove-wood and lumps of coal were all mingled in indescribable confusion.

JANUARY 10-JANUARY 14: Mostly head winds.

JANUARY 15: . . . All afternoon and evening the breeze held and what a glorious run we had. The little ship carried all her canvas well and logged her ten knots for twelve solid hours . . . put life into everyone . . . an exhilarating sensation as we skimmed along touching only the high places, with the breeze humming and thrumming through the rigging and the frothy spray dashing across our bows, and when the moon came out bright and clear in the evening the beauty of the picture was complete.

JANUARY 16-17: Head winds.

JANUARY 18: . . . There is a tremendous sea running and wave after wave comes following us, towering over our heads almost as high as the mainmast and threatening to fall in a deluge over our stern. . . . She is rolling to such an extent that the deck is a continual wash.

JANUARY 19: Day was so fine and mild that our passengers seemed more lively . . . our skipper appeared on deck today for the first time . . . he looked thin and worn out.

JANUARY 20-21: Light fair wind, four knots.

JANUARY 22: Good stiff sailing breeze. Seem to have struck N.E. Trades.

JANUARY 23: Quiet night; five knots.

JANUARY 24-28: Steady breeze; averaging six knots.

JANUARY 29: . . . everything set . . . made 171 miles, the biggest day's run yet . . . about 1800 miles to make but if this breeze holds we will do it inside two weeks. (Actually they were ten!)

JANUARY 30-FEBRUARY 1: Still steady N.E. Trades.

140

FEBRUARY 2: Sunday. Very warm ... in the evening I got the guitar out and we had a little concert ... broke off when a school of porpoises came alongside.

FEBRUARY 3-4: Head winds.

FEBRUARY 5: ... Caught shark. A shark's tail nailed to the end of the jibboom will always bring fair winds ... and we were not long getting it into position. Sure enough the breeze hauled to the N.E. and ... we were able to lay our course due east for Cocos ... we are in the latitude of it but 18 degrees to the westward. If this breeze would only hold we could make the island in another week.

FEBRUARY 6-7: Tropical deluges ... seem in the doldrums.

FEBRUARY 8: A steady breeze from the S.E. all day and it looks as if we have struck the S.E. Trades. If this is the case we will stand on south till we reach the line and then put about and lay our course for Cocos.

FEBRUARY 9: Good winds.

FEBRUARY 10: ... a dead calm ... terrific heat from an almost cloudless sky and as it is almost fore and aft with our course we have not even the shade of the sails. The pitch is boiling and bubbling from the seams and the planks are almost hot enough to roast. ... Now we are in the doldrums it may take weeks to reach Cocos.

FEBRUARY 11: Calm by day, light wind at night.

FEBRUARY 12: ... Sun boiling overhead. We saw a turtle asleep about half a mile off ... lowered a boat ... drew up to him without waking him, drove the harpoon into him ... tonight we had curried turtle and rice.

FEBRUARY 14-15: Calm interspersed with tropical showers.

FEBRUARY 16: Heavy rain ... filling our tanks ... I rigged a tent over our bunks in the dory on deck and we expect to be able to sleep there in any kind of weather.

FEBRUARY 17: Mostly calm.

FEBRUARY 18: ... All day long we have not moved a foot. A box we flung overboard this morning is not a quarter of a mile away this evening. Everybody is feeling depressed by the stagnation.

FEBRUARY 19: Heavy rain.

FEBRUARY 20: Calm till noon; then 4-knot S.E. breeze.

FEBRUARY 21: ... In our dogwatch on deck Jim Blackwood was giving us his experience with Mrs. Young, the Nanaimo clairvoyant, who said, "I see an island away out to sea and it looks like a tropical island ... coins and bars of gold buried in the rock. ... You will go there and you will be successful in finding the treasure." He then told her who he was and . . . about Cocos Island and on producing charts of the island she pointed out the spots where the treasure was buried.

FEBRUARY 22-23: Rain!

FEBRUARY 26: . . . We are beginning to lose hope of ever getting there and the reaction is evident in the tempers of the crew. . . . We are certainly in a hard place to make any headway being in the belt of calms with a westerly current continually heading us off.

FEBRUARY 27: Breeze at last. Seems like S.E. Trades.

FEBRUARY 28: . . . we are now within a thousand miles of the island, our position today being 99:45 W., and 1:14 S.

MARCH 1: Squally.

MARCH 2: . . . today are 1:19 north of the line. Unless we strike a better slant of wind we will never see Cocos. The big mistake was when we came down this way instead of hugging the coast.

MARCH 3: . . . It is lucky we have plenty of water and provisions for it looks as if we are about to repeat the experience of the Ancient Mariner or the Flying Dutchman.

MARCH 4: A large sword-fish was hanging around this morning about fifteen feet in length and with a sword fully four feet long.

MARCH 5: . . . A turtle speared and hauled on board. They have astonishing vitality as his heart continued to beat long after the meat was cut up and in the pot.

MARCH 6-7: Hot, fairly good winds.

MARCH 9: Another day rolling in the swell. . . . The skipper said today two more weeks of this . . . and he would head up for Victoria. About 6 p.m. a breeze from the N.E.

MARCH 10-13: N.E. breezes.

MARCH 14: The N.N.E. breeze holds steady but is drawing more to the eastward is doing us no good . . . today we were put as the last resort at making spun yarn. This is certainly no pleasure trip. I have not known an idle five minutes in my watch on deck since I have been on board as the mate (Gus Whidden) can always find something for us to do.

MARCH 15: Light baffling winds.

MARCH 16: Little progress on our course.

MARCH 17-18: Rain.

MARCH 19: . . . We passed a number of small pieces of driftwood

142

and leaves today in a fair state of preservation which seems to indicate that we are nearer land than we expect.

MARCH 20: Not a breath of wind but a tremendous swell in which the old tub wallowed till she dipped her scuppers in the sea and her decks were awash . . . boiling hot sun . . . makes existence almost unbearable.

MARCH 21: . . . We had a tremendous downpour of rain . . . and some of us enjoyed the luxury of a shower-bath. Standing under the foot of a sail it is delightful to get deluged with the warm water pouring in cataracts on the decks.

MARCH 22: Light fair winds.

MARCH 23: Drifting.

MARCH 24: . . . We were busy today cleaning and repacking the biscuits. They were damp and mouldy a month ago and they are much worse now. The weevils are beginning to show themselves now so I don't know what they will be like by the time we get back to Victoria.

MARCH 25: Rain. Wind increased in afternoon.

MARCH 26: . . . At last we have run out of the nineties and today our position is Long. 89:57 W., and Lat. 5:15 N., so we are only 175 miles from Cocos.

MARCH 27: We must be only a little over a hundred miles from Cocos. Saw today a stick of hewed timber about three feet square on the end and twenty feet long with an iron staple on the upper side and it floated so light it could not have been long in the sea.

MARCH 28: Tonight we have hove to for fear of missing the island. I was aloft just before dark having a good look for it but there is nothing in sight. Rain.

MARCH 30: Easter Sunday. Every little while someone is aloft anxiously scanning the horizon but nothing appears. Warm. No wind.

MARCH 31: We overhauled the boats today getting them ready to go ashore on the land we have yet to find. No wind in night; N.E. by day.

APRIL 1: Light head winds.

APRIL 2: Head winds.

APRIL 3: We are only about thirty miles from the island but it seems impossible to get there. It is certainly trying on a person's temper.

APRIL 4: Tomorrow at noon the sun will be directly overhead and the altitude will be ninety.

APRIL 5: No wind. A strong current has set us into Long. 86:36 W. so that we are now 25 miles east of Cocos. We are beginning to think Cocos Island is a will-o-wisp or there must have been a violent volcanic eruption.

APRIL 6: Rain; little wind.

APRIL 9: All hands were oiling and painting their oilskins today as they have become sadly leaky with constant use.

APRIL 11: Tonight a stiff squall from the S.E. and if it will only hold till morning we shall be where the island ought to be. Whether or not we will find it there is a doubtful question.

APRIL 12: Still no land. I expect the next move will be to put about and make for the mainland and correct the chronometers.

APRIL 13: Sure enough last night 'bout ship and head for the mainland. At dark discovered upper topsail yard sprung. Breeze steady S.E.

APRIL 14: At 5:30 a.m. sent down topsail. Then fished the yard with six 3 by 4 scantlings twenty feet long, splicing them to the yard and binding them with three chain lashings on each side of the tie. Heavy to hoist.

APRIL 15: Headed east all day.

APRIL 16: At daybreak sighted sail; first we have seen for a couple of months. We hauled up to her; she shortened down. She proved to be a Danish barque just out of Panama. A tremendous squall of wind and rain struck us before we reached her and when we were beside her it was almost impossible to hear. However they managed to tell us our longitude was 88:00 where we were reckoning on 84:30. This makes our chronometer about thirteen minutes slow instead of six, the old error. A rare piece of luck as it would have taken us a couple of weeks to go to the mainland and return. Besides it is a rare occurrence for a vessel to be found in these waters. We are now about seventy miles from Cocos and as we have a good beam wind we will likely sight the island by daybreak.

APRIL 17: AT LAST! we have reached Cocos and the anchor is down. When we came on deck at midnight we could make out the faint loom of land in the moonlight but so far away that we could not be sure of it. We shortened down and approached slowly and at daybreak there was the island standing out plain and rocky about six miles off. All hands on deck, overhaul the cables, cast the

144

anchors and all was bustle and excitement. When all was clear every glass on the ship was in constant use. . . . We ran past Wafer Bay and rounding a small island anchored in Chatham Bay about half a mile from shore. As soon as the anchor was down we put our boats over and nearly all hands went ashore. Dense vines and steep hillsides . . . forced us to stay near the beach. Found coconut trees . . . soon regaling ourselves. We raced about like a party of schoolboys so elated did we feel after seeing nothing but sea and sky for over 100 days. Every here and there along the beach are large boulders on which are carved the names of the ships that have visited the island with dates ranging from 1740 to the present day.

APRIL 18: Mr. Gilbert, the mate, Mr. Enyeart, Raub and Tommy all took their blankets and a cooking outfit and went around to Wafer Bay to prospect. (Others did necessary work on ship.) Mr. Powell and Shef shot a pig. The hogs were landed by Captain George Vancouver and have run wild. They are small, and when dressed look more like a small deer than a hog.

APRIL 19: Gus and I had our leave ashore this afternoon. We rowed along the shore and had not gone far when we saw two pigs running down the cliff through the bush. There was a tremendous surf running but I managed to jump ashore with the rifle leaving Gus to keep the dory off the rocks. I shot two pigs but getting them aboard again was the hardest task. I had to take one pig at a time, wade into the surf with him, brace my feet good and solid and when the dory came rushing in on top of a roller, heave the pig into it and scramble up out of the water before the undertow could carry me off. On returning to the ship we heard shore party expected they had located some of treasure from action of the instruments.

APRIL 20: Geo. Forbes and I took dory and went in chase of huge sunfish . . . about fourteen feet long and about ten feet from tip to tip of his fins. Put two shots in him but he only jumped a bit. Went to waterfall and filled water-jugs . . . We have been eating bananas and drinking lemorade all afternoon. We had a delightful swim in the creek without any fear of sharks. The shore party have hopes . . . instruments have acted in four different places. The captain was just now telling me he had worked up the chronometer error and found the instrument twenty-one minutes forty-eight seconds slow. No wonder we could not find Cocos with such an error.

APRIL 21: ... I have been busy all day getting water. There is a waterfall about a quarter of a mile away in which I have rigged a spout to throw the water about six feet from the rocks. At high water we can go in under the spout with the boat so this afternoon I brought off five boatloads which filled two of our largest casks. It is only on the quietest days we can load it owing to the very heavy surf.

APRIL 22: After breakfast the captain, the second mate and I pulled over to Dead Man's Point to examine a cave he had noticed in the cliff. Mr. Powell and I landed and climbed up the back of the cliff. At the top of the cliff made a line fast to tree and threw end over cliff. I slid down to the cave the skipper had noticed. It was only a small hole. ... Hard climb hand over hand back to the top. A sailor is buried just here on the top of the cliff but however they got the body up is a mystery to me. A piece of broken cross is standing over the grave. Later chasing pigs I got nearly eaten to death by little red ants and when I reached the beach I was in such torment that I stripped and rushed into the surf regardless of the sharks. There are millions of these little ants on every tree and bush and their bite is almost as bad as a bee's sting. ... In the afternoon the skipper and I pulled round to Wafer Bay with supplies for the shore party. Found them at the bottom of twenty foot hole. Instrument gave strong attraction here in space four feet square but they are now giving up this place after reaching hardpan.

APRIL 23: ... to Wafer Bay with supplies. Jim Blackwood has found the identical spot where Mrs. Young told him he was to find the treasure — tallies in every way. Instruments also show attraction there so they are starting to dig. Coming back along the coast just as we reached the mouth of a cave a huge wave sent us booming through a natural arch for about fifty feet and there we found the cave expanded into a huge roomy chamber, so large in fact that we felt the ocean swell very little. We pulled around it but it was too dark to see the most remote corners. We had some trouble getting out through the surf but managed it without swamping our boat.

APRIL 24: Went ashore here in Chatham Bay and cleared off the spot where seven crocks of gold are supposed to be buried "on the bank of the creek fifteen feet to the left of a big flat rock"! In afternoon towed raft round to Wafer Bay. Found part of shore gang boring holes in new location and others in the spot Jim had located.

This latter looks to me the most likely spot yet. The instructions for the position of the Devonshire treasure all point to this spot and the ground in the immediate vicinity is dug up and tunneled in all directions by former searchers. . . . Tonight the captain took me into his cabin and showed the letter of instruction Keyton (Keating) had left and also a copy of the chart given to his brother Tom Hackett.

APRIL 25: . . . beautiful day but there is a heavy nor'west swell into the bay and the old *Blakeley* lies wallowing in the trough of the swell rolling worse than she did at sea. . . . Picked over potatoes in the forenoon. . . . In afternoon Gus and I took dory . . . we pulled halfway round island . . . landed at sheltered cove on south side . . . number of coconut trees growing on the beach so we loaded our boat with coconuts in place of the pigs we had gone out for.

APRIL 27: I have been forced to stay on board today with cramps. The boys started off with the boat in the morning to look for pigs and they continued till they had made the circuit of the island. I would have given a good deal to be with them to complete my chart of the island.

APRIL 28: Captain, Gus and I went to . . . Little Bay. This is where the village (Gissler's) stood formerly but today there is only the remains of one galvanized iron house. Travelled up the creek half a mile looking for a spot that would fit directions on the map but found nothing. On the flat near the beach we found a big hole dug by a former expedition, and it seemed to correspond with the bearings for Boat Rock. There are two little hills here and the foot of either of them might be where they buried the treasure. Instruments found strong attraction here.

APRIL 29: Worked today at Wafer Bay looking for Devonshire treasure.

APRIL 30: One gang working in Wafer Bay for Keyton's treasure, four of us on Devonshire location. Our shaft down to twenty feet . . . muddy . . . formation changed from rock to blue clay and now to hard red clay. Water is pouring in so fast we will have to abandon it. Suffering from heat and headaches.

MAY 1: Very hot and sultry. Not a cloud or breath of wind to temper blazing sun. Another month of this would be the death of most of us.

MAY 2: A little cooler today. We shifted a great quantity of earth from the face of the cliff. This face has certainly slipped down a long time ago. I expect another day or two will put us down to the mouth of the old tunnel if such a thing ever existed . . . another week will determine our fate. However we will have a good swim tonight, treasure or no treasure and that in itself after a hard day's work in the sun is worth a fortune.

MAY 3: We had several tests today with Mr. Gilbert's gold-finding instrument and proved to the satisfaction of all that it will not work with Gilbert or anyone else. Tests: We laid my watch and purse containing gold and silver coins on sand and buried them. Pointed for Gilbert space fifty feet square to find them in . . . spot located by instrument 33 feet from the spot. Likewise later test. Gilbert says his nerves are bad and would like another test but I think he himself is satisfied the instrument is no good. . . . Enyeart will acknowledge his instrument is attracting to something other than gold. (Tests at Beacon Hill Park before voyage had seemed satisfactory.)

MAY 4: I had intended pulling round the island today (Sunday) but there was too much wind from the S.E.

MAY 5: Working in the shade of the cliff all forenoon so not so hot but in the afternoon the sun beat down on us most cruelly.

MAY 6: A hard day's work but nothing special in sight.

MAY 7: . . . finished at Little Bay and found nothing. At our location (Wafer Bay) they had long consultations and decided to make open cut and sink shaft a little deeper.

MAY 8: We all started at Wafer Bay this morning but seemed labor in vain. Gilbert has been wanting to give it up ever since I came ashore (April 29). Mr. Whidden asked us our opinion and as we all seemed willing to quit he and Gilbert and Enyeart went aboard to interview the skipper. When they returned they had decided to sink the shaft a few feet deeper and then abandon it. In the afternoon it came on to rain heavy and we were forced to quit work. As the tide was high we went down to the beach and fired off a couple of sticks of dynamite and dead fish came up by the dozens. We had no boat so we stripped and into the water to gather fish. Sometimes wading, sometimes swimming, then being carried away by a sudden rush of the swift current . . . again diving for those that sank in the deep water. We had an hour's excellent sport. Then the work commenced as we turned to and cleaned and scrubbed the fish and by dark we had a half cask salted down for our return trip.

148

MAY 9: In the morning we baled out our shaft and bored a hole in the bottom about eight feet deeper. Passed through the red clay and into brown clay and sand. I panned out a shovel full of it in the creek and found it full of mica but Mr. Enyeart claims there is gold in it too. We brought some of it away for analysis — and that finished our search for treasure on Cocos Island!

In the afternoon we went into the bush and cut a spare topsail yard. We found one near the bank so we cut it and slid it down into the creek at high-water and floated it down to the beach. When we got it into deep water we had rare sport riding the log and ducking each other.

The captain was ashore today to see if all were satisfied to quit and as we all agreed we are to go on board tomorrow.

MAY 10: All hands aboard and Cocos Island is deserted again. In the morning we took all that remained of our dynamite, about a case and a half and placed it under the cliff where we had been working. We put about ten feet of fuse in it and ran about 300 yards. The report was terrific and seemed to shake the island to its foundations. The whole face of the cliff was torn down and ... the vines for fifty yards around were stripped of their leaves.

It was low water at noon so I spent the time measuring the holes we had dug and estimating the amount of work done. In the afternoon we took the remainder of our gear aboard ... and towed out the spar. Everybody glad to be aboard again.

MAY 11: The morning being fine Gus, Geordie and I took the dory and started to pull round the island but when we rounded the S.W. point we found a strong westerly breeze blowing and making it impossible to proceed further. We put about and were about three miles from the ship when a squall from the N.E. caught us and for the remainder of the trip we had excitement enough to satisfy anybody. The wind came down in howling gusts and the torrents of rain drove into our faces with such force that we could not face it. For a time it was a struggle to keep from being driven on the rocky beach where the heavy surf would soon have made an end of us. At last we managed to make the lee side of an islet and hung on there till the wind shifted a little to the eastward. By this time a tremendous sea was running but we knew our chance was now or never so we put out and by good luck and good management we got on board safely.

Here we found everything in excitement. The vessel had dragged close in shore and she was now heaving and pitching with both anchors down and threatening to snap the cable in the heavy swell. Suddenly the wind shifted, blowing straight out of the bay and the captain decided to up anchor and run out to sea.

We struck awnings and then all hands on the windlass and "heave away"! The anchors broke out easily, a couple of hands loosened the jibs and topsails and away we stood for home.

Then we had a risky piece of work getting our boats on board but we accomplished it with no more accident than staving in a plank on one of the sealing boats.

By dark we had all sail she could carry on her, the anchors fished and catted and the boat secured for the night. We then went to supper to the cheerful music of homeward bound.

Our greatest regret in leaving so suddenly is that we are forced to leave behind our half barrel of fish and we have only about half a dozen bunches of bananas where we intended having a shipload.

MAY 12: Light wind. Island still in sight about 40 miles to the east.

MAY 15: (After two good days) a miserable day, rain and thunder showers and squalls all day. In dogwatch the spar fished on the way down began to snap.

MAY 16: Strong S. wind. In morning cutting strips to fish broken yard. At noon the roping on the leash of the mainsail carried away so there was a whole afternoon's job repairing that in the pelting rain. Our gear is all so old and rotten that we will have steady work patching and mending. Every time I go on deck there is something to repair. The worst of it is we have no new gear to reeve off in place of the old. Most of the orders for supplies were cancelled by the managers. When they find the ship will be delayed about a month by their senseless economy they will realize they have been cutting expenses at the wrong end.

MAY 17: Gale; heavy seas.

MAY 18: Calm. Drifting back E.

MAY 19: Hard day's work patching upper topsail yard. . . . With upper sail on she is not rolling and pitching so much and is doing a couple of extra knots an hour. Blowing hard.

MAY 20: Soft light southwest winds make the air feel soft and balmy, like the eastern Indian summer. (Kirkendale's youth spent in Ontario.)

MAY 21: . . . owing to our rotten gear we have to nurse the old packet like a baby and take no chances with the weather. Squalls of wind and rain. Afternoon steady N.W. breeze.

MAY 22: Continual succession heavy squalls . . . wind all from W. dead ahead.

MAY 24: Victoria Day and here we are five thousand miles from home without a bell on. At last we have had a change and have had a beautiful day without a drop of rain.

MAY 25-27: Light fair winds.

MAY 29: The last of our bananas disappeared today.

MAY 31: We are now only 150 miles west of Cocos after three weeks hard graft. We ate the last of the potatoes today. Showery, squally all day.

JUNE 1-3: Wet, poor weather.

JUNE 4: Steady 4-knot breeze from the south so that we can just lay our course W. by S.

JUNE 7: Winds shifting to all points of the compass. About 3 a.m. the heaviest rain storm I have ever seen, a driving S.W. wind and plenty of thunder and lightning.

JUNE 8: Fine day for a change. A poem on "The man from Spokane" was found nailed to the mast this morning and has been the joke of the ship today.

JUNE 9: Last of the tea. Current takes us to 97 W.

JUNE 10: About as miserable a watch as I ever put in last night. Rain fell in torrents, wind shifting to all points of the compass. Our oilskins are almost worn out with constant use and we are never dry.

JUNE 12: Good steady blow from S.S.W., making five or six knots westward. Rainy weather too monotonous for endurance; all suffering from rheumatism, lumbago or the blues.

JUNE 14: Rain, rain, but the situation has its humorous side. When the steward was bringing breakfast along to the cabin the vessel gave a heavy roll just as he reached the companionway and away went a mixture of steward, stew and hotcakes and dishes into the lee scuppers. Raub came sailing along with a broom to sweep up the mess and as he stepped on the greasy deck she gave another roll and before he knew what had happened he had landed on the deck and followed Long Jim into the scuppers. It was the neatest drop I have ever seen on a ship's deck.

JUNE 15-16: Steady, heavy rain.

JUNE 18: We cut up a new forestay sail to patch our old sails today as we have run short of canvas. Rain all night; wind dead ahead.

JUNE 22: Wind from all points. Rain.

JUNE 23: For the first time in months 24 hours without rain.

JUNE 24: Spent the whole day patching the flying jib. Very light winds.

JUNE 25-26: Dead calm. Calm and showers.

JUNE 27: We saw an exciting chase between a dolphin and a flying fish. The latter was about a foot out of the water and the dolphin with about half his length out of the water about six inches behind him. They travelled about a hundred yards and then it was all over like a flash of lighting. The dolphin had the reputation of being the fastest fish in the water and so he must be if he can go as fast as a flying fish can fly. Calm.

JUNE 28: Calm and showery. Little breeze from S.W. in a.m.

JUNE 29: We are getting to be a floating hospital — three men with running sores. Three knot breeze from S.S.W. Heavy rain.

JULY 1: Oatmeal now so mouldy we cannot use it and the flour too sour to rise. Light breeze . . . can make true course.

JULY 2: Enough wind to keep moving.

JULY 3: Dead calm.

JULY 4: The sunset tonight the most brilliant I have ever seen. Not only was the sky red in the west and in the east but the whole heaven from horizon to horizon was a brilliant mass of coloring, so bright that the reflection made the water appear like blood. Everybody aboard said it was the finest sight they had every seen.

JULY 5-7: Good 8-knot wind.

JULY 8: Dead calm till next dawn.

JULY 9: Good breeze. This is the most like the N.E. Trades of anything we have seen. If it is we could be home in a month.

JULY 14: Nights colder. Have to don underclothing again. Last night was the first time I have worn a coat in five months.

JULY 16: The wind is blowing from due north. We will bring up in Honolulu if this holds much longer. There is a driving sleet coming with the wind. Our rice has given out and the bread is so sour we can hardly eat it.

JULY 17: Heavy blow; driving rain. We have not seen the sun for two days but she is directly overhead today on her journey south.

JULY 18: Blowing heavy and still raining. She is almost jumping her spars out.

JULY 19: The same heavy weather . . . very cold . . . always wet.

JULY 21: Got a sight of the sun for the first time in 6 days and found our position just 20 miles different to that by Dead Reckoning. Remarkably good judgment in a run of 1,000 miles.

JULY 22: Today we saw one of the birds known as Frisco Pilot. They are seldom seen below 30 N. and it seemed like a glimpse of home to see him again. Canned soup gone and today we use the last of our milk.

JULY 23: Overcast, but no rain. Good day's work on the rigging.

JULY 25: The heaviest blow we've had. Sea breaking over her continually but we are driving her through on N.W. course.

JULY 26: Sugar done; beans finished. All we have left is musty flour and salt pork and beef. Light rain. Sea and wind moderating.

JULY 27: We are now north of the parallel of Frisco but are making rapidly to the west. If this wind does not change soon we will be forced to put about and beat up for the cape and goodness knows when we will get in.

JULY 28: Wind has shifted. Rippling along with a 6-knot S.W. breeze. Day beautifully bright and everybody happy and cheerful.

JULY 29: Fine breeze continues. We broke up the boxes of mouldy biscuit. In middle of boxes were some good biscuits and we had a splendid feed on biscuits and hot water. I think we can find enough biscuits to keep us going till we get in.

JULY 31: We are now 630 miles from the cape and we will make that in five days at this rate. It will be none too soon as we are beginning to feel the effects of hard living and starvation. Still we are expected to get the ship scrubbed and polished and painted for entering port.

AUGUST 1: Fog. Light S.W. wind. Heavy ground swell.

AUGUST 3: We have seen several pieces of kelp drifting about which makes us think that we are closer than we think by our chronometer.

AUGUST 4: Breeze steady. Made 150 miles, course E.

AUGUST 5: About 4 p.m. I saw a few white specks to the N.E. and immediately sung out the welcome cry of Land Ho! Soon the fog thinned out and we could distinctly make out the high land behind Clayoquot about thirty miles away. If the present breeze holds we will be in Victoria tomorrow. Getting anchors ready and chains overhauled.

AUGUST 6: The breeze died out and we have had hardly a breath since last evening. When day broke we recognized the land just above Alberni and a little later saw Cape Beale. I know as soon as the ship touches the dock we will all make a break for a restaurant and have a "feed."

AUGUST 7 (although on this day even the steady Kirkendale makes a mistake and titles it July 7!): The wind fell completely during the night and this morning we were tumbling and rolling in the heavy swell off Flattery. At daylight the tug *Magic* came along and offered to take us to Victoria for $100. Captain refused but was then called down by mate and we all followed suit . . . so he hoisted the flag for tug to return. In less than an hour we had the tow line fast and sails all stowed for harbor. Skipper of the *Magic* passed us a few spuds and some tea and sugar and Raub caught a salmon and we made a luxurious breakfast. We stopped at the quarantine but we all passed muster. Reached the Outer Wharf about 5:30 p.m. and I was the only one aboard well enough acquainted with the harbor to take her in. We went right up through the bridge and tied up at Spratt's Wharf amid a storm of cheers from the crowd assembled to welcome us home. No one could account for our delay and we had been given up for lost so it was no wonder people rejoiced to see us return even though we came empty-handed!

L'ENVOI

SUCH WAS LIFE IN THE DAYS OF SAIL. Such was the price paid by the men who made up the crews of such ships. Fortunately for the memory of such men, in spots all round the world are to be found clubs like the Thermopylae, pledged to keep in mind and on record, the contributions of the courageous, hard-working sailormen of yore.

*   *   *

So the years have gone by. Most of those whose yarns have filled the pages of this book have gone their way, new men have signed on. Yet still today their successors gather to listen to some tale of the sea. Sometimes even now there is still some personal experience to be heard of the almost-vanished days of sail but more often the account is of a recent scientific expedition that has sought to explore some new aspect of the eternally mysterious and challenging ocean, or some new means of interlocking the economy of man and the sea.

And still at year's end this amiable crew foregathers, as it has done each year since 1933, at an annual Christmas banquet, and toasts the memory of the sea and the ships and men that sail on it.

Now and again there has been the old salt who has felt called on to celebrate the occasion in verse, as the following poem shows.

SONG OF THE SEA
(tune — Old Lang Syne)

by CAPTAIN C. P. KINNEY

Once more we meet on the good old ship,
The voyage has just begun,
We'll sail her as we did before
Until the voyage is done.
We've had salt beef and good plum duff
And heard tales of the sea,
And may we all meet here again
On the old Thermopylae.

Chorus

The old Thermopylae, my boys,
The old Thermopylae,
We wish her luck and give three cheers
For the old Thermopylae.

Skippers of the Thermopylae Club
(to 1950)

1932-1938	Alexander McDonald
DECEMBER 1938	C. P. Kinney
SEPTEMBER 1940	Charles Goring
JUNE 1943	J. A. Philipsen (died February 1944)
MARCH 1944	McDonald moved from Chief Officer to Skipper
APRIL 1947	C. F. Gray (acting)
OCTOBER 1947	Frank Baylis (acting)
MARCH 1948	Frank Baylis
FEBRUARY 1949	J. B. White
JANUARY 1950	Charles F. Gray

Shipmates of the Thermopylae Club
(to 1950)

OCTOBER 21, 1932
Pre-organization

F. V. Longstaff
P. L. James
F. W. Kemp
W. T. Thorne
J. A. Philipsen
Thos. McKenzie
C. D. Neroutsos
A. M. Davie
W. T. M. Barrett
A. McDonald
H. D. Mathias
N. P. Blandy
O. P. Parker

NOVEMBER 16, 1932
(first dog-watch)

D. J. Butler
F. Robertson
W. De Gruchy
J. M. Grant
M. A. W. Bridgman
George Kirkendale

JANUARY 12, 1933

Harvey B. Nicolle
Frank Wilson
W. G. Garrard
H. Adlem
B. H. Robson

FEBRUARY 8, 1933

J. G. Clack
J. A. Barron
Thomas McCallum
A. Faire
F. W. Hearle
R. S. Johnson
A. D. Barff

JUNE 14, 1933

J. G. Thorburn
E. H. Pope
E. D. Smoothy

OCTOBER 11, 1933

Douglas Barff
W. T. Wilson
W. J. Ward
Granville Cuppage
H. W. Price
T. A. Simmons
S. Harrison
J. C. Campbell
S. J. Spark
R. Garratt

NOVEMBER 8, 1933

Ben Axhorn
A. T. R. Bullen

JANUARY 10, 1934

J. Kirkendale

158

FEBRUARY 14, 1934

C. Sainty
J. Walker
Victor Jacobsen
C. P. Kinney
F. Evans
H. P. Eldridge
J. Peacock
J. Kemp
T. Miller, surgeon
G. Longfield
Alan McGregor

MARCH 14, 1934

F. C. Adams
Stewart G. Clarke
Ben B. Temple
B. L. Robertson

MAY 7, 1934

Wm. Halgren

NOVEMBER 14, 1934

B. Sivertz

DECEMBER 12, 1934

F. W. Taylor
G. A. Thomson
W. A. Turner

FEBRUARY 13, 1935

J. J. Moore

OCTOBER 9, 1935

Seymour Biggs

APRIL 8, 1936

D. S. Scott
F. L. Elliott

S. W. Brock
R. W. D. Stanger

FEBRUARY 10, 1937

Angus McDonald
Wm. Goulden

MAY 17, 1937

Charles Goring

FEBRUARY 1938

P. Shandley

MARCH 9, 1938

George Seeley

OCTOBER 12, 1938

R. A. Read
F. Baylis

DECEMBER 14, 1936

M. D. A. Darling
W. G. Nettleship
C. T. Beard
G. Lee-Warner

MARCH 1939

George Deaville
E. Davidson
Charles Hensley
J. H. Blake
— Parks (*St. Roch*)

NOVEMBER 15, 1939

G. D. Robertson
H. A. Larsen (*St. Roch*)
Henry Passmore

159

FEBRUARY 21, 1940
J. D. Waddington
Dr. Harper
J. J. Mathieson (holder of
Norwegian, British and U.S.
papers)

FEBRUARY 12, 1941
F. G. Pell
— Potter

MAY 1943
C. F. Gray
Captain Wingate
J. Thorpe

APRIL 12, 1944
R. Morrison

MAY 10, 1944
Oscar Scarf

JANUARY 10, 1945
E. J. Ruxton
J. C. de Balinhard
F. Riley
A. W. Hammond
R. Kiley

FEBRUARY 14, 1945
F. C. Johnson
W. Linton
— Elkington

JUNE 13, 1945
F. W. Webb
(sailed on *Thermopylae*)
N. A. Beketov

APRIL 9, 1947
H. L. Cadieux
F. C. Theobald
F. E. Fredette

AUGUST 18, 1948
H. Halderson

NOVEMBER 1948
S. J. Cole
G. D. Miles
J. Barber

NOVEMBER 1948
Harry Bilton

FEBRUARY 1949
H. Watkins

MARCH 1949
Fred Jones

SEPTEMBER 1949
William Gregory

Many of these men were master mariners but due to difficulty in establishing all entitled to this honour I have chosen to omit it entirely.

To any former shipmates, whose names, hidden amid the varied pages of the log, I may have overlooked — my apologies. But may you too enjoy meeting again these companions of long ago.

Index